The task of moving from the te
faithful exposition is challenging.
aims to help the Bible teacher to ob
and prepare to convey its significa

In this way these volumes often do more than the weightier
technical commentaries. It is like having the guidance of an
experienced coach in the wonderful work of rightly handling the
word of truth.

John Woodhouse
Principal,
Moore College,
Sydney, Australia

Angus MacLeay takes us through this important letter with
enormous clarity and care. This is an outstanding resource;
essential reading for all looking to study, teach and feed on
1 Timothy.

Sam Allberry
Assistant Pastor,
St Marys, Maidenhead and Author of *Lifted*

It's my observation that many evangelical ministers have been
reluctant to preach 1 Timothy because they fear some of the more
controversial issues that it covers will divide their congregations.
Sadly, this means that the prevailing culture then dictates what
people think about, for example, the role of women in the church.
Angus' book will help ministers to bridge those troubled waters
and tackles all the issues with clarity, sensitivity and wisdom. If
the growing feminisation of the church is to be challenged and
men encouraged to step up and take the lead, then we need
1 Timothy to be preached, taught and modelled in our churches.

Carrie Sandom
Author, Speaker, Women's Instructor, Cornhill Training Course, London ,
Associate Minister for Women and Pastoral care, St John Church,
Tunbride Wells, England

We ignore the Pastorals to our loss and peril. The elderly apostle is looking down the tube and preparing Timothy and Titus and us for the post-apostolic age. Once again we are greatly indebted to Proclamation Trust Resources for their series on teaching different books of the Bible. After Angus Macleay's outstanding contribution on 1 Peter his new book on 1 Timothy does not disappoint – the same excellent standard is maintained. Difficulties are faced. Practical application is realistic. The text lives. My immediate reaction was to resolve to make 1 Timothy our next study book for our mid-week groups and/or the basis of the next sermon series.

Jonathan Fletcher
Minister,
Emmanuel Church,
Wimbledon, England

North India desperately needs men and women who will preach and teach the Bible faithfully and PT's Teaching series is of great value in encouraging them to do just that. They are just what we need. We have found the books of great help in English and eagerly anticipate the day when they will be available in Hindi also.

Isaac Shaw
Executive Director,
Delhi Bible Institute

TEACHING
1 TIMOTHY

From text to message

ANGUS MACLEAY

SERIES EDITORS: DAVID JACKMAN & ADRIAN REYNOLDS

PT RESOURCES

CHRISTIAN
FOCUS

Copyright © Proclamation Trust Resources 2012

ISBN 978-1-84550-808-1

10 9 8 7 6 5 4 3 2 1

Published in 2012
by
Christian Focus Publications Ltd.,
Geanies House, Fearn, Ross-shire,
IV20 1TW, Scotland, Great Britain
with
Proclamation Trust Resources,
Willcox House, 140-148 Borough High Street,
London, SE1 1LB, England, Great Britain.
www.proctrust.org.uk

www.christianfocus.com

Cover design by www.moose77.com

Printed and bound by
Nørhaven, Denmark

Contents

Contents — expanded

SERIES PREFACE

It has sometimes been said that 1 Timothy is a key New Testament book for understanding the shape and structure of church life, and that, though we live in different times from 1st century Asia, the Word of God – as always – cuts through and addresses extremely contemporary church issues. Whilst there is much truth in this, Angus explains very clearly in this book that 1 Timothy is about so much more than church order. Indeed, such a topic sounds woefully dull and uninteresting. Rather, Paul's concerned letter to Timothy has, at its heart, a call for godly living which will cause the gospel to be displayed in Ephesus and to have an impact on the surrounding society.

Angus' contribution to our growing series is thus a very important and timely one. 1 Timothy is a book which many might feel they want to preach, but sense they are ill-equipped to do so, dealing, as it does, with so many contemporary issues. This volume will be a great help to the preacher or Bible study leader, giving them confidence in the inspired Word of God and practical help as they obey the call to preach the Word faithfully.

The first section contains basic 'navigation' material to get you into the text of 1 Timothy, covering aspects like structure and planning a series. The 'meat' of the book then works systematically through the major sections of 1 Timothy, suggesting preaching or teaching units, including sermon outlines and questions for Bible studies. These are not there to take the hard work out of preparation, but as a starting point to get you thinking about how to preach the material or prepare a Bible study.

Teaching 1 Timothy brings the number of published volumes in the series to ten. We are encouraged at how the series continues to develop and the positive comments from people that really matter – those at the chalk face of Christian ministry, working hard at the Word of God, week in week out, to proclaim the unsearchable riches of Christ.

Our thanks go, as ever, to the team at Christian Focus for their committed partnership in this project.

David Jackman & Adrian Reynolds
Series Editors, London, March 2012

AUTHOR'S PREFACE

Over the course of a year preachers inevitably find themselves handling various parts of the Bible. However, following advice from a number of respected church leaders, I have adopted the practice of giving particular attention to one Bible book each year. This has the benefit of giving a focus and depth to sermon preparation over a longer period than usual. Spending more time on one book often leads to greater clarity in understanding the original setting as well as in thinking through points of application. Hopefully it is therefore an enriching experience both for the Bible teacher and the congregation.

During 2010, my special focus was 1 Timothy. Its message about the importance of keeping an outward gospel focus is always relevant but there were other points that particularly resonated. Amidst my involvement in various Church of England General Synod Committees which related to the issue of women in the episcopate, it was helpful to be reminded of the way the apostle Paul roots his teaching about women in creation (1 Tim. 2:12, 13). Amidst the uncertainties of the world financial markets, it was good to think through a Biblical perspective on money (1 Tim. 6:17-19). Though we are not resident in first century Ephesus, nevertheless as Christians the issues we face remain the same.

I prepared and preached during 2010 with no thought of turning this material into a written format. However, as with my previous book in this series, 'Teaching 1 Peter', it was due to illness that I found that the Lord provided me with the space and time required to reflect and write. On Tuesday 19th April 2011 I suffered a cardiac arrest. The Lord mercifully provided people around me at the time, my wife Sue and son Jamie as well as two staff colleagues, Robin Lochhead and Michael Dormandy, who were able to give immediate assistance. The following evening whilst I was still in a coma, almost two hundred members of the St. Nicholas church family gathered for prayer, and in God's goodness slowly over the following days I was enabled to make a complete recovery. In gratitude for their prayers, love and support, this book is dedicated to the St. Nicholas church family whom I have had the privilege of serving since 2001.

In fact, such was my recovery that I was only signed off work for a further month. However, the offer of a three-month period of study leave combined with gentle and persistent persuasion from the church leadership that I should take this opportunity meant that I now had the space and time to devote myself to writing. I was delighted that Adrian Reynolds and David Jackman at the Proclamation Trust felt able to trust me with this project and I have been very grateful for their wisdom and insight over the months that followed, whilst recognising that any errors in exegesis and infelicities in language must remain my own responsibility.

I would also like to put on record my gratitude to various staff members at St. Nicholas, Margaret Marshall, Pippa Halpin and Melita Rozario and at the Proclamation Trust Crystal Williams, who have all been involved in various ways in typing up this manuscript. I am also grateful to Wycliffe Hall, Oxford, where I trained for ordained ministry, in enabling me to make use of their library. Particular thanks must go to my family Sue, Rachel and Jamie, for their unwavering love and support during the days when I was critically ill and each day since.

My prayer is that you will find this book to be of assistance in enabling you to be a faithful and engaging preacher of 1 Timothy.

Angus MacLeay
February 2012

For the St. Nicholas Sevenoaks Church family
with gratitude for your prayers
on the evening of
Wednesday 20th April 2011.

How to Use this Book

This book aims to help the preacher or teacher understand the central aim and purpose of the text, in order to preach or teach it. Unlike a commentary, therefore, it does not go into great exegetical detail. Instead it helps us to engage with Paul's own themes, to keep the big picture in mind, and to think about how to present it to our hearers.

1. 'Part One: Introducing 1 Timothy' gives some background to the letter, including context, purpose and structure. This material is crucial to our understanding of the whole book and will shape the way we preach each section to our congregations. This preliminary section also divides the book into preaching units, each of which will form a successive chapter in the book. Also in this section is a brief discussion of issues that preaching 1 Timothy raises together with a rationale for why we *should* preach and teach this rich epistle.

2. Each chapter then takes a preaching unit one at a time and follows the same pattern:

Structure of the chapters which follow

Each chapter within this book is based on a relatively short portion of 1 Timothy and follows a consistent structure, specifically geared to help the preacher to get to grips with the text in order to teach it. Some brief comments follow which will help explain how this process seeks to serve the purpose of proclaiming God's Word.

Listening to the text

Context, structure and observations

Careful attention to the text is critically important. What we think is there, or what our systematic theology tells us is there, may not necessarily be present at all. An attempt has been made to look as sensitively as possible at the text in order first to understand the context of that part of 1 Timothy. It is often useful to consider why a passage has been included by Paul or to consider links with preceding and following passages. An attempt has also been made to look at the structure of the text under consideration, since sensitivity to the way in which Paul has set things out can often be invaluable in helping the preacher to see how to tackle the passage and what the significant message of that particular section is. Finally, consideration is often given to the words which Paul uses and, where appropriate, when they are used at other points in the epistle. Such observations are not meant to be exhaustive, but provide helpful insights which should be borne in mind before tackling the passage.

Exposition

The intention here is not to produce a full, technical commentary on 1 Timothy, but simply to give an explanation of how the text fits together so that the preacher can see the main ideas within the passage. The titles and headings aim for clarity and are not chosen with the pulpit directly in mind.

From text to teaching

By this point we should have got to grips with the essentials of the passage and now have a 'text to explain'. However, if that is the end point, our sermon is likely to be presented like a lecture or commentary. To preach a passage we need to move from a 'text to explain' to having a 'message to proclaim'. To assist in this process a number of steps can be identified.

Get the message clear

The main concern here is to nail down the essential message of the text. A helpful way to do this is to identify the big idea or the main theme. We can then consider what main question(s) the text addresses. If our preaching is to be engaging then our sermons must answer questions, and these should be the questions addressed by the passage. It is good to state the big idea of the passage in one succinct sentence, and then to express this as a question. The preacher can go on to show why the big question is important and relevant for listeners.

Engage the hearer

Point of contact

It is important to give careful attention to the introduction to a sermon. Rather than start immediately in the Bible, my preference is to start with ordinary life situations and then raise the issue to be addressed by the Bible passage. Starting the sermon in this way provides a 'hook' so that people can see that this sermon and Bible passage may have immediate relevance to their lives. A good introduction should therefore establish a point of contact with the listeners and connect with the big idea or the big question of the passage.

Main illustration

Rightly handled, illustrations can provide windows within the structure of our sermons and bring light, clarity and understanding. My own general rule is that each point needs to be carefully illustrated and applied so that those listening can more easily understand what Paul is saying to them. However, illustrations often date quickly and may arise out of the preacher's own observations, reading, experiences and setting. I have tried to assist the preacher by providing one illustration which helps to explain and throw light on one of the central teaching points in the passage, but preachers should think carefully about illustrations which are relevant for their own congregations.

Application

The purpose of including this section is as a reminder that 1 Timothy contains a message which is to be preached so that lives are changed as a result. Of necessity my application is fairly general and would need to be sharpened up considerably for use in any given situation. Readers will see that each of the application points links to a teaching point made in the exposition earlier within the chapter.

Proclaiming the message

A preaching outline
A title and preaching outline based on the exposition are suggested.

Other preaching possibilities
This section is designed to assist in the process of deciding how to divide up 1 Timothy. Various possibilities are suggested indicating where and how one passage can be linked with another. Also, although the assumption is that preachers will want to tackle 1 Timothy in an expository fashion moving from passage to passage through the whole of the letter, from time to time themes are suggested which it might be profitable to explore.

Leading a Bible Study
The final part of each chapter includes a Bible study with some suggestions for questions which could be used by the leader. The Bible study works through four logical steps:

1. Introduce the issues – an opportunity to think about one of the main issues which will be raised by the text in order to engage the group members.

2. Study the passage – questions designed to help the group to dig into the text for themselves.

3. Think it through – questions designed to help members reflect on what they are discovering in the Bible passage.

4. Live it out – questions designed to sharpen the application of the lessons learned from God's Word.

Part I
INTRODUCTORY MATERIAL

Getting our bearings in 1 Timothy

Introduction

For many congregations 1 Timothy is a neglected part of the New Testament. This may be for a number of reasons which will be explored in more detail below, but perhaps mainly it is because many preachers will naturally want to shy away from the controversial passage relating to women's ministry in the local church (1 Tim. 2:11-15) in order to avoid the potential collision between the apostle Paul's teaching and the expectations of modern culture. However, as our congregations navigate their way amidst the surroundings of this culture it is clear that there are many benefits from undertaking an expository series of sermons or set of Bible Studies on this letter.

At the heart of 1 Timothy is a concern for godliness within God's household in order to enable the truth of the gospel to be displayed to the world (see 3:15). There is also a drive to bring a church infected with false teaching back to full health and vigour. Wherever, therefore, the gospel has been obscured and worldly behaviour has become pervasive it will be found that 1 Timothy has a striking relevance and application. If you want to preach on a book which will call the church to focus more on the gospel and godly living in order to advance the gospel within your community then 1 Timothy is an extremely appropriate choice.

The apostle Paul

The book starts with an introduction from Paul, an apostle of Christ Jesus. Within 1 Timothy there are several passages which are autobiographical and they helpfully pick up two distinct aspects of the apostle's life and ministry.

First, 1:12-16 refers to his conversion. The narrative of these events is found in Acts 9 which corroborates the material found here. We are informed that Paul had been a blasphemer, a persecutor and a violent man (1:13) such that as he looks back towards the end of his ministry, perhaps around A.D. 63-65, he is able to describe himself as the worst of sinners (1:15, 16). Yet having been involved in persecuting the church, his life was turned around through the amazing grace, mercy and patience of the Lord (1:13-16). Paul glories in knowing God as his Saviour (1:1, 2:4, 4:10) and at several points simply overflows in praise to the God who has shown such undeserved love (1:17, 6:15, 16).

Second, 1:12 and 2:7 reveal that not only was Paul converted, but that he was also given a special commission by the Lord Jesus Christ. He was entrusted with the gospel message (1:11) and appointed in particular to be an apostle to the Gentiles/nations so that the whole world could learn about the Lord Jesus Christ through his ministry of preaching and teaching, which again links in with the conversion narrative in Acts 9:15. Paul therefore has a particular burden to ensure that the Church at Ephesus, which he had been involved in planting, should also embody that same vision to take the gospel to the world.

Timothy

The letter is written by Paul to 'Timothy my true son in the faith' (1:2). Again the passages in Acts flesh out the details. Timothy first appears at Lystra in modern-day Turkey in Acts 16:1 and the best explanation of Paul's reference to him as 'my true son' (1:2) or 'my son' (1:18) would appear to be that Timothy had come to follow Christ through the ministry of the apostle Paul, as is further suggested in Philippians 2:22. Second, he is soon found accompanying Paul on his missionary journeys (Acts 16:3; 17:14f; 18:5; 19:22; 20:4) and as time goes on he is often sent ahead by Paul as an envoy (1 Cor. 4:17; 16:10; 1 Thess. 3:6). Third, such a close working partnership develops that Paul can refer to him as his co-worker (Rom. 16:21) and several of his epistles are sent jointly from Paul and Timothy (2 Cor. 1:1; Phil. 1:1; Col. 1:1; 1 Thess. 1:1; 2 Thess. 1:1; Philem. 1:1). Fourth, we learn that Timothy's ministry is noteworthy for his concern both for Christ's interests and the welfare of the churches he serves (Phil. 2:20, 21). Rather than being concerned for his own security or reputation he has given himself to the cause of Christ, the gospel and the local church. Mention is sometimes made of Timothy's timidity (2 Tim. 1:7) and his physical weakness (5:23) but these verses need to be set in the context of a wholehearted ministry of service to the Lord Jesus Christ, which includes imprisonment for the sake of the gospel (Heb. 13:23). Timothy may indeed need encouragement from Paul to face the demands of ministry and the hostility that sometimes accompanied this role, but as 1 Thessalonians 3:2 reminds us, he was a dear brother and God's fellow worker in spreading the gospel of Christ as he sought to strengthen and encourage the early Christian churches in their faith.

The Church at Ephesus

When Paul writes this letter, Timothy is based in Ephesus (1:3). He had been sent there in order to sort out particular problems that had been developing. As Paul's representative his task was to call the church back to the apostolic teaching that it had originally received. Though the letter is primarily written to his trusted friend, it is also written to be heard by that church as is evidenced by the use of the plural 'you' in the final verse of the epistle (6:21 'Grace be with you'). This church had been planted by the apostle Paul (Acts 19) and he committed himself to building it through an unusually long stay in the city of two years (Acts 19:10) (and see 1 Cor.16:8 where he talks of a door for effective work having opened up at Ephesus) so that he could see it firmly established. His relationship with the church can be seen in his farewell speech to the church leaders at Ephesus when he was passing nearby on a subsequent missionary journey (Acts 20:17-35). Speaking to the elders, whom he also refers to as overseers or bishops (Acts 20:17, 28 – the same terms used at 1 Tim. 3:1; 5:17), he speaks of his labours in Ephesus before highlighting the danger of false teachers appearing from within that leadership (Acts 20:29, 30) which is the very issue which later causes him to write 1 Timothy (1:3; 6:3). Life for Paul at Ephesus had not been easy (see 1 Cor. 15:32 where he speaks of battling with wild animals – a reference to the hostile reception he received within his Ephesian ministry) yet there had also been support from people such as Onesiphorus (2 Tim. 1:18).

The other material which specifically relates to Ephesus is Paul's letter to the Ephesians, though this may well have been a circular letter which was not exclusive to that city. Moreover, at the end of the New Testament there is the material in Revelation 2:1-7 in the Lord Jesus' letter to the Church at Ephesus. Significantly, amidst all the good things to report, the Lord highlights the serious problem that the church had lost its first love. Somehow, though continuing in service to Christ in various ways, they were no longer marked by a great passion for Him – other things were obscuring the gospel. This piercing diagnosis can also be applied to the Church at Ephesus when 1 Timothy was written. Though there are certainly many good things to report, somehow the gospel of our Lord Jesus Christ was no longer central and part of Paul's encouragement to Timothy is to ensure that the gospel shapes the life of the church far more than it had been doing.

The presenting issue

The issue which Paul is especially concerned about and which motivates him to write to Timothy is flagged up right at the outset at 1:3. Some people were teaching 'other doctrines', fulfilling the warning of Acts 20:29, 30. This teaching will be explored in greater depth within the exposition, but the passages within 1 Timothy which are particularly relevant in gaining an understanding of what was being taught include 1:3-7; 4:1-3; 6:3-5 and 6:20, 21. The church appears not to have plunged into doctrinal heresy in an outright rejection of the gospel, but the effect of the prevailing teaching was that the glorious gospel was being obscured through a focus on law (1:6; 4:3) which led to legalism, asceticism and infighting within the church (1:4, 6; 6:3-5, 20) and the further danger of people wandering from the faith (1:6; 5:15; 6:10, 21). The result was an inward-looking church characterised by distinctly ungodly behaviour, which had no doubt caused the church to have a poor reputation within the surrounding community. The fact that Paul begins and ends his epistle with such a clarion call for Timothy to sort these issues out (1:3; 6:20f) gives the clearest indication that this is why he has been forced to write.

However, it would be a mistake to think that the letter is simply a negative reaction to a set of challenging circumstances. The positive thrust of Paul's writing can be seen right at the heart of the epistle at 3:15 with his call for godly living which will cause the gospel to be displayed within Ephesus. This positive thrust is developed in many ways as he seeks to re-shape the church so as to make an impact for the gospel on the surrounding society.

The structure of 1 Timothy

Sometimes the structure of a book of the Bible is obscured from view because of chapter divisions or the translators' uninspired headings within the book. Yet if a clear structure can be discerned it can be of enormous benefit in aiding understanding as the author's thought-flow is unpacked. It can be especially valuable to the preacher. This is particularly true for 1 Timothy.

There are five main sections within the book which approximate to a chiastic pattern with the first and final, second and fourth sections dealing with very similar themes working up to a central section which reveals the main positive thrust of the letter.

Section 1 1:1-20

Section 2 2:1-3:13

Section 3 3:14-4:16

Section 4 5:1-6:2

Section 5 6:3-21

The beginning (1:1-20) and end (6:3-21) both start with a clear reference to the teaching of other/different doctrines (1:3; 6:3) and each section develops in different ways a necessary response to the danger by focusing on the gospel message. In the first section, with the false teaching characterised as legalistic ('it's all about what we do') the focus of the gospel is all about what Christ has done at the Cross (1:15). In the final section the false teaching is characterised as ultimately materialistic ('it's all about what we have' 6:5, 9, 10) whereas the focus of the gospel is all about what Christ will give to us on His return (6:14, 15). These two distinct responses are even headlined in the opening verse of the epistle as Paul refers to God our Saviour, as well as to Christ our hope (1:1).

Working towards the centre of the letter, the next sections (2:1–3:13 and 5:1–6:2) primarily deal with the issues within the church family that Timothy must specifically resolve at Ephesus. In the second section, the church is to be more focussed on the proclamation of the gospel and on living godly lives and this is especially applicable for its leadership. In the fourth section, the church needs to act as a caring and godly family with the opening verses highlighting the relationships between church family members as being like fathers, mothers, brothers and sisters (5:1, 2). The church family needs to care for widows by honouring them as mothers, for its elders by relating to them as fathers and to masters as brothers. This fourth section is carefully linked by the use of the word variously translated as 'honour' or 'respect' at the beginning of each sub-section (5:3, 17; 6:1).

The third section stands at the centre of the letter and runs from 3:14–4:16. Most of it is centred in terms of personal instruction to Timothy about what he is to do until Paul is able to join him (see 3:14; 4:13). The focus of the section is to highlight the importance of godly living and the gospel. It is established as the main priority for Timothy in his dealing with the church (3:15) and it is to be underlined through his own personal and public example, the section concluding with a call to watch his life and doctrine.

Discerning this structure provides an understanding of the flow of the book as Paul seeks to resist the false teaching (sections 1 and 5), promote godly behaviour in order to sort out particular behavioural issues within the church family (sections 2 and 4) and encourage Timothy to be a faithful leader of the church as he models godliness and keeps a focus on the gospel in his teaching (section 3). 1 Timothy therefore provides tremendous material to the church facing false teaching and how to overcome it through a fresh understanding of the gospel. It also provides plenty of guidance to help a church to function appropriately. Ultimately it provides a clear pattern for the work of the church leader in seeking to lead the church family in the right way. Without Timothy's faithful leadership the church was likely to run aground (1:19). Therefore this letter helps us to see that the vitality of the church is closely linked to the sort of leadership that Paul envisages Timothy will undertake.

The outline of 1 Timothy

The following provides a brief outline of the main divisions of 1 Timothy which are explored within this book. As has been argued, Paul operates with a clear structure in mind. Further sub-divisions of each section will be developed within each chapter, so this is a fairly simplified outline offered to help understand the structure of the epistle.

Introduction (1:1, 2)

(1) Responding to false teaching by living in the light of Christ's cross (1:3-20)

1:3-7	The danger of false teaching
1:8-20	The response to legalism

(2) Restoring the church: focusing on the gospel and godliness (2:1–3:13)

2:1-7	Characteristics of the gospel-centred church
2:8-15	Characteristics of the gospel-centred member
3:1-13	Characteristics of the gospel-centred leader

(3) Reminding Timothy of the importance of godliness and the gospel (3:14–4:16)

3:14-4:5	The priority of godliness and the gospel
4:6-16	The example of godliness and the gospel

(4) Restoring the church: focusing on living as a loving church family (5:1–6:2)

5:1-16	Honouring widows
5:17-6:2	Honouring elders and masters

(5) Responding to false teaching by living in the light of Christ's return (6:3-21)

6:3-10	The danger of false teaching
6:11-21	The response to materialism

Questions for studying 1 Timothy

Each sub-section includes a set of Bible Study questions which may be of some assistance. In addition, the following questions may also be useful for a group which has read through 1 Timothy together in its entirety, as a prelude to the study of individual passages.

1. What is the key issue that is facing Timothy and the church at Ephesus?

2. How is this issue to be addressed by Timothy

    … reactively? (what must he challenge or resist?)

    … proactively? (what must he aim for?)

3. What is Paul especially looking for within the church leadership at Ephesus?

4. What is Paul especially looking for within the church membership?

5. How does Paul want the church at Ephesus to relate to the surrounding society?

6. What is the main personal challenge to Timothy within the epistle?

7. What are the links between godliness within the church membership and godliness within the church leadership?

1. Why we should preach and teach 1 Timothy

What are the reasons why 1 Timothy is not taught more often?

There are a number of reasons why this book is not preached more often, some of which are based on misunderstandings about the content and the structure of the epistle.

In many situations the particular presenting issue of the false teaching being experienced at Ephesus seems remote. Our problems by and large don't involve detailed discussions about myths and genealogies (1:4) and therefore the teaching may seem distant and irrelevant.

Many preachers feel uncertain about the structure of the book. Why is Paul teaching about leadership in different ways in chapters 3, 4 and 5 rather than looking at this subject in a more coherent way? Is there a pattern within the book and clear thought-flow from one section to another? Why are there two brief sections on handling money within chapter 6 when it would seem more appropriate for them to be placed together? Failing to find adequate answers to these sorts of questions makes the book more of a challenge for the preacher.

Preachers may have been misled by some older commentaries which seem to suggest that 1 Timothy was a manual of church order with instructions about worship, appointing leaders, caring for widows etc. These instructions appear to be fairly muddled, with no particular order, which is frustrating for the preacher. However, the main issue is that church practice is dynamic and understanding 1 Timothy as a church order manual makes the letter feel obscure and outdated.

Finally, the issue which will certainly cause difficulties for some preachers and congregations is the clear teaching against women being appointed to authoritative teaching roles over the main congregation (1 Tim. 2:11-15). How can this position be squared not only with the rightful equality provisions of contemporary society, but also the changed positions of many denominations which now authorise women as ministers, elders, preachers, etc.?

Not all these reasons may carry the same weight, but cumulatively they represent a powerful disincentive to spend time preaching through the whole epistle. It is useful, therefore, to set out the positive benefits of teaching the book.

What are the reasons why it is particularly useful to preach 1 Timothy?

In Paul's second letter to Timothy he states that, 'all scripture is God-breathed and is useful for teaching, rebuking, correcting and training in righteousness ...' (2 Tim. 3:16), and we need to be reminded that, as God's Word, each book, including 1 Timothy, will speak powerfully to each generation regardless of how remote and irrelevant some may consider it to be. However, there are more reasons even than this that reveal why 1 Timothy will often be highly relevant to today's church.

The church at Ephesus had absorbed teaching that was both legalistic (1:7) and materialistic (6:5) and as a result was characterised by infighting and squabbling and had become inward-looking. As a consequence it was making little positive impact on the surrounding society – and indeed the reputation of the church within the community was at a particularly low ebb. When stated in this way, it can soon be recognised that the teaching in this letter is anything but remote. Many of our churches face the same struggles of seeking to resist moralism and/or materialism. Many of our churches have become inward-looking. Many of our churches and denominations do not enjoy a positive reputation because of our behaviour as Christians and, as a consequence, struggle to make much of an impact upon our society. 1 Timothy speaks directly to such situations today.

Linked to this , like the church at Ephesus rebuked by the Lord Jesus at Revelation 2:4, many of us have lost our first love. Primarily this relates to our love for the Lord Jesus Christ and our love of the gospel but it may also be linked to our love for Christ's followers. In many situations our devotion to Christ and love for his people have become routine and perfunctory, rather than real and passionate. 1 Timothy speaks directly to such situations today.

Next, we may well feel concerned about the state of Christian leadership. We may be dazzled by gifts but correspondingly confused when either prominent church leaders or local church youth leaders become embroiled in scandal due to falling into sinful patterns of behaviour. The famous Scottish preacher Murray McCheyne said that his people's greatest need was his holiness and, though simple, godly, Christ-like living may seem ordinary and mundane, nevertheless it is the vital building block for any Christian ministry. Paul's first letter to Timothy speaks directly to such situations today.

Finally, in many churches the reality is simply that the undergrowth of weeds has gradually grown up and obscured the beautiful flowers of Christ, the gospel and godly living. With the passing of time these have gradually disappeared from view and a version of the gospel without its power to transform and change has been imbibed. Once again 1 Timothy speaks to such situations today.

Of course there will be many other reasons for preaching any book of the Bible but those set out immediately highlight that 1 Timothy is far from remote or irrelevant. It challenges a church that has drifted. It helps the church to re-focus on the gospel. It encourages the sort of godly behaviour that should mark the church and which should have an impact on the surrounding community. It is therefore worth careful study and application to our churches today.

2. Ideas for preaching and teaching a series on 1 Timothy

Introduction

One of the practical issues facing the preacher committed to the expository method concerns the division of a book of the Bible into appropriate sections for preaching. A number of factors must be considered:

+ Would the congregation benefit more from an overview of the letter taking only a few sermons or by allocating plenty of time to the detail of the letter?

+ How long would the congregation be able to cope with a particular series?

+ Are there any particular constraints which need to be borne in mind, e.g. a time frame such as an academic term, church diary constraints due to special events or holidays, preaching allocations (if there is more than one preacher available)?

A number of possible series are listed below. In each case the intention is to work with the structure and flow of the epistle.

Series 1: 5 sermons

+ Sermon 1   1:1-20

+ Sermon 2   2:1–3:13

+ Sermon 3   3:14–4:16

+ Sermon 4   5:1–6:2

+ Sermon 5   6:3-21

Clearly the aim here is to provide a brief overview of the whole letter. The outline uses Paul's five sections as its main structure. If the fellowship is considering doing a series of midweek Bible studies on 1 Timothy, a relatively short amount of time giving an overview from the pulpit might help the Bible Study group leaders and members to see how the main themes of the letter are developed. This format may lend itself to a weekend houseparty where there is an opportunity for sustained teaching on one Bible book.

Series 2: 11 Sermons

- Sermon 1   1:1-7; 6:20, 21
- Sermon 2   1:8-20
- Sermon 3   2:1-7
- Sermon 4   2:8-15
- Sermon 5   3:1-13
- Sermon 6   3:14–4:5
- Sermon 7   4:6-16
- Sermon 8   5:1-16
- Sermon 9   5:17–6:2
- Sermon 10   6:3-10
- Sermon 11   6:11-21

This series is the selection developed within this book. This is roughly how I chose to preach through 1 Timothy myself. It gave me scope to get into a fair amount of detail whilst not getting too bogged down so that the congregation could retain a clear idea of the flow of the epistle. Naturally, there were frustrations in being unable to spend quite so much time on some parts as one would have wished.

Series 3: 19 sermons

- Sermon 1   1:1-7; 6:20, 21
- Sermon 2   1:8-11
- Sermon 3   1:12-17
- Sermon 4   1:18-20
- Sermon 5   2:1-7
- Sermon 6   2:8-10
- Sermon 7   2:11-15
- Sermon 8   3:1-7
- Sermon 9   3:8-13
- Sermon 10 3:14-16
- Sermon 11 4:1-5
- Sermon 12 4:6-10
- Sermon 13 4:11-16
- Sermon 14 5:1-16
- Sermon 15 5:17-25
- Sermon 16 6:1-2
- Sermon 17 6:3-10
- Sermon 18 6:11-16
- Sermon 19 6:17-21

The obvious advantage of working slowly through the material is that the details can be covered, though there could also be the danger of missing the wood for the trees. If undertaking this more substantial exposition, you might wish to consider breaking the series at one or two points in order to make things more manageable and in order to provide a brief overview each time you return. The breaks could come for example after sermon 9 and sermon 13 enabling you to work with the grain of the main building blocks of 1 Timothy identified previously.

Learning from Paul about preaching

Before we proceed to look at the text of 1 Timothy in detail it would be helpful for the preacher to be reminded of Paul's own view of preaching from this epistle.

Preaching flows out of a passion for Christ and the gospel

At various points we see Paul gripped by the message of grace and the wonder of knowing God (1:15-17; 6:14-16). His praise of God is not strictly speaking required in his argument but the words about God tumble out indicating his passion. Genuine preaching that warms the congregation and causes hearts to burn (Luke 24:32) must come from hearts already on fire for Christ and the gospel. The preacher, like Paul, may need to remind himself of the glory of the gospel of grace as Paul does at 1:12-15 in order to burn with passion for Christ in the pulpit.

Preaching is based on a clear message about Christ

At 2:3-7 Paul gives a concise explanation of the way preaching the gospel to the nations/Gentiles flows from a clear doctrinal conviction about the nature of God, the person of Christ and substitutionary atonement. Preaching which does not proceed from these doctrines will always lack conviction and substance.

Preaching requires appropriate gifts but also hard work

The distinctive qualification of the overseer is that he is able to teach (3:2). Though deacons are required to be capable of holding on to the deep truths of the faith, there is a recognition that without the distinctive gifting of being able to teach they are not able to fulfil the main leadership and preaching role. However, though the overseer/elder needs this gifting, the chief mark which Paul highlights as deserving of respect is that they direct the affairs of the church wisely and work hard, indeed labour, at preaching and teaching (5:17). This is underlined by the quotation from the Old Testament in which the preacher is compared to the ox laboriously treading out the grain (5:18). It may not be a flattering picture for the gifted preacher to be viewed as an ox but the point is that preaching is hard work and deserves all our strength and mental application.

Preaching must be based on a platform of godly living

One of the distinctive contributions of 1 Timothy is the amount of material devoted to the need for godly living for the church leader and preacher. Not only is it an essential qualification that the church needs to consider in appointing the preacher (3:1-7), but in the ongoing work training in godliness is vital, as witnessed in the teaching to Timothy himself at 4:6-8. The way we live does affect the way we preach and how we are heard.

Preaching requires a devotion to the truth

Alongside the previous point we see that, as the climax of the personal instructions to Timothy, he is told to watch his life and doctrine as through these means he will be the agent of salvation (4:16). It should be noted that this comes at the end of a section where Paul has used verbs of great intensity to underline what is required of Timothy. He is to be devoted to this public ministry of reading scripture, preaching and teaching. He is to be diligent, giving himself completely to the task and he is to persevere (4:13-16). This commitment to the truth is undergirded at the very end with the stirring call for Timothy to guard the deposit (6:20), such is its value. The preacher must be devoted above all to the Word of God.

Perhaps in preaching a series on 1 Timothy it would be advisable for the preacher to ensure that he has listened to its teaching and applied it to himself first before opening up the treasures within the letter! At the same time, this teaching in 1 Timothy can also be very beneficial to members of the congregation in helping them to see how they can be praying for and encouraging their preachers.

Part 2

Responding to False Teaching

1 Timothy 1:1-20

1. A church in danger (1:1-7; 6:20-21)

Introduction

At the beginning and end of this epistle the presenting
issue concerning the church in Ephesus is revealed. People
teaching false (NIV) or different (ESV) doctrines had arisen
perhaps from within the church family just as Paul had
warned (Acts 20:29,30). This was not something which
Paul could permit to continue and so as an apostle under
the command of the Lord Jesus Christ (1:1) he writes
to Timothy (1:2) whom he had led to a personal faith in
Christ many years previously (Acts 16:1ff.). This teaching
must be opposed (1:3) and the truth must be guarded
(6:20); otherwise many will find themselves wandering
from the faith (1:6; 6:21). Taking a look at both the
beginning and the end of many of Paul's letters is often
a fruitful way of identifying some of the main concerns and
this is particularly the case with 1 Timothy and therefore

it is recommended that 6:20,21 be included in the opening exposition.

Listening to the text

Context, structure and observations

Context
It is simply worth highlighting that 1:3 provides us with the setting of this epistle. It identifies the geographical location (Ephesus) as well as the historical context (Paul is currently not in prison but is able to travel freely as is also picked up at 3:14 and 4:13) whilst also providing the theological background for the whole letter (the existence of people teaching different doctrines which needed to be resisted).

Structure
There is a clear chiastic structure within 1:3-7 as set out below:

A.   1:3,4a People teaching different doctrines

     B.   1:4 Result of false teaching = controversy

          C.   1:5 The goal of genuine Christianity
                    = faith leading to love

     B.   1:6 Result of false teaching = wandering
            from the faith

A.   1:7 People teaching different doctrines (law)

Identifying this structure is enormously helpful in preaching the passage as it identifies the main issues immediately.

Observations
In 1:1 we are informed that Paul is writing at the command of God our Saviour and of Christ Jesus our hope. It may be

helpful to observe that whereas Paul counters the legalism of the false teachers ('it's all about what we do') by reference to God's saving events in the coming and crucifixion of our Lord Jesus Christ (1:15), at the other end of the epistle Paul counters the materialism of these teachers ('it's all about what we can get now' 6:5) by reference to God's future saving events (our hope) in the return of our Lord Jesus Christ (6:14). Seen in this light, the terms used by Paul to describe the Godhead in 1:1 are not accidental but clearly link in with the required response, revealing that the ultimate answer to these different doctrines is found within the Godhead.

In 1:2 we see that the letter is specifically written to Timothy but the final verse of the epistle is directed to the whole church by the use of 'you' in the plural form ('grace be with you' 6:21). This indicates that though it is written primarily for Timothy it is to be overheard by the whole church family, so that together the various issues that face the church can be revealed and addressed.

The conjunction of faith and a good conscience is found at several points (see 1:5, 19; 3:9; 4:1, 2) and indicates an important theme for the epistle – repetitions often underline or highlight the significance of the words.

Exposition

Utilising the chiastic structure found within 1:3-7 our exposition will trace the three different parts of the structure in order to unpack what is contained within the first main paragraph.

What was the problem? (1.3, 4a, 7; 6:20)

From amongst their number (Acts 20:29, 30) certain teachers had been teaching false or different doctrines which must be addressed by Timothy. Both the opening and concluding sections of the epistle identify this issue (1:3; 6:3). What were they teaching? It involved a devotion to myths (1:4; 4:7) – mere speculation based on anecdote, rumour or imagination without any secure footing in the truth. It also involved an interest in genealogies (1:4) – perhaps a desire to compare which stream of tradition you belonged to in order to assess whether you were really 'in' or not. Such myths and genealogies result in what is 'falsely called knowledge' (6:20) though it is in reality nothing of the sort. However, perhaps the most important clue to the content of their teaching is found at 1:7. These people wanted to be teachers of the law and had descended into legalism (see 4:3 for some examples) though they had no real sense of the danger into which they were leading the church. Perhaps their teaching derived from reasonable motives – 'Ephesus is such a sinful and wicked city that we must provide really clear guidelines to new Christians concerning how they are to behave in order to keep them from becoming contaminated.' Yet in proceeding in this direction they had no idea what they were doing and what would be its consequences for the church and the gospel (1:7).

As a general point, it is important that these teachers of different doctrines are not overvilified in our preaching; otherwise we make them look so ridiculous and remote that we remove any possibility that such teaching could be a challenge to the churches in our generation. As a result the teaching of 1 Timothy itself becomes less relevant and more remote. Seeking to understand, and to a certain extent be sympathetic to their reasoning alerts us to the fact that this could be a current issue for our church and highlights the importance of Paul's handling of the issue in this letter.

In summary, these teachers may have known their Bibles well but they majored on minors and somehow they had neglected that which was really important – Christ and the gospel. As with the diagnosis of this same church at Rev. 2:4 they had forgotten their first love. Now it had become all about what you *do* (law 1:7) and what you *know* (knowledge 6:20). And yet they didn't really have knowledge because Christ was no longer at the centre of this church – it had become all about them.

Seen in this light we can see why Paul instructs Timothy using strong language. 'Command' these people not to teach these things (1:3). 'Guard' what has been entrusted to you (6:20, a reference to the gospel which had been entrusted to Paul 1:11). Action is required to combat this dangerous state of affairs.

What were the results of this teaching? (1:4, 6;6: 20, 21)
Their teaching led to controversies (1:4) which had clearly become extremely heated and had generated an enormous amount of friction between church members (6:3-5). It is also characterised as 'meaningless talk' (1:6) or 'vain discussion' (esv). At the end of the letter it is referred to as 'godless chatter' (6:20) or perhaps even more forcefully as 'irreverent babble' (esv). As with a car which has the engine running at full throttle but which is not in gear, there is tremendous noise, heat and friction but no forward movement to the intended destination.

Yet hand in hand with such ungodly behaviour came an even more critical fall-out from the false teaching – people were wandering away from the faith (1:6; 6:21). At several points Paul highlights the danger by using a number of different words: 'wandering' from, 'swerving' from or 'abandoning' the faith (1:19; 4:1; 5:15; 6:10) and this is clearly an important pastoral consideration which lends urgency to the charge to Timothy. We can easily imagine people attending the church or home group in Ephesus and being appalled at the behaviour highlighted at 6:3,4 and, as a result, slipping away.

What is the solution? (1:4, 5)
Paul identifies the solution by sharing the need to re-focus on the really important things.

Re-focus on the gospel (1:1, 2, 4)
Paul starts by focusing on the gospel which brings salvation and hope (1:1) and which delivers grace, mercy and peace (1:2). Further, he reminds Timothy that God's work is promoted not by arguments but by faith in Jesus Christ (1:4). Salvation will not come through greater obedience to the law (1:7) or superior knowledge (6:20) but only through ongoing trust and faith in the Lord Jesus Christ, as Paul will go on to demonstrate through his own personal experience at 1:12-17. The church must not cover up or obscure this glorious gospel message but must be a pillar and foundation of the truth (3:15) enabling the truth of the gospel to be on display for all to see. Faith in Christ must be central!

Re-focus on godliness (1:5)
The goal of Paul's command at 1:3 is not just to correct the false teachers but to see God's work actively promoted at Ephesus in the lives of believers. The goal or aim is love (1:5) – a contrast to the arguments and squabbles that the church was currently enduring. And how are such loving relationships to be achieved? It is through a 'pure heart' (avoiding the pollution of the world, and behaviour unbecoming to a Christian, for example) a 'good conscience' (being able to stand before Christ in contrast to those who have acted in such a way that their consciences had become seared and as a consequence

were unable to discern God's ways 4:1, 2) and a 'sincere faith' (through a genuine, ongoing, loving trust in the Lord Jesus Christ in contrast to those who had abandoned the faith or made shipwreck of it 1:19; 4:1). The call to show love or to know how to conduct oneself in a godly way within God's household (3:15) is central to the letter.

Paul therefore wishes to see a church re-focusing on the gospel and godliness or, as he expresses it both here and at Galatians 5:6, 'the only thing that counts is faith expressing itself in love.' The rubble of the false teaching and the rubbish that has been left behind must be removed in order that the church can be rebuilt on its proper foundations. In rebuilding and reclaiming the church at Ephesus the central themes will be the glorious gospel of our Lord Jesus Christ, received by faith in Him and the response of godliness, revealed in love.

In summary, Paul has given a clear diagnosis of the problem that the church faces with the rise of their false teachers (1:3, 7). He has also given the prognosis – of where such teaching will lead and its disastrous effects on the whole church family in terms of ungodly behaviour and people wandering from the faith (1:4, 6). Finally, like any good doctor, Paul has also prescribed the best medicine in order to bring healing and wholeness through refocusing on the gospel and its effect: godliness, faith and love (1:5).

From text to teaching

Get the message clear

Big idea (theme)
We must guard against the danger of legalism and people wandering away from the faith, through focusing on the gospel and godly living.

Big questions (aim)

Preaching or teaching on this passage should answer the following questions:

1. What is the danger facing the church when Christ and the gospel are no longer central?

2. What are the hallmarks of such a religion?

3. What is the goal of genuine Christian faith?

Engage the hearer

Point of contact

Over a period of time a house can fall into disrepair, sometimes without the occupier even noticing. Cracks can appear on the brickwork, damp patches in the bedroom and perhaps a door or window needs replacing. Gradually things can deteriorate unless action is taken. Similarly over a period of time a healthy church can also deteriorate, often without anybody realising what is happening, such that urgent remedial action is required to bring it back to where it should be. The church at Ephesus had fallen into disrepair only some fifteen years after being planted by the apostle. Churches in our own day can also drift into a state of disrepair (of course I am not referring to the fabric of the building where the church family may gather each week) such that urgent action is required.

Main illustration

The text refers to people wandering from the faith. It is easy to think of situations where people have wandered off course – perhaps a yacht being driven off course by wind, tide and currents and sailing precariously close to rocks. Or perhaps walkers out on the hills not bothering to use maps or a compass and finding that, as the mist descends, they are

now far away from their intended destination. The danger
at Ephesus was that people were already wandering off
course and it is of course a danger for our churches today.

Application
The preacher will want to highlight that the problem at
Ephesus with false teachers was not confined to that day.
Evangelicalism, with its focus on God's Word, can be
particularly susceptible to descending into legalism, vain
discussions and controversies. It is easy for us to focus on
knowledge (6:20) for its own sake and for us to measure
our standing by our own performance. Our vision of
Christianity then falls entirely on ourselves – it's all about
what we do or what we know. Yet that is the very situation
which is of such concern to the apostle. An evangelicalism
that has gone to seed in this way needs the remedy of
1 Timothy and a re-focusing on the gospel and godly living.

Linked to this is the danger of getting embroiled in
long arguments, controversies and heated exchanges about
secondary issues which become time-consuming and deflect
from the centrality of the gospel. Such controversies may
even be the means of people wandering from the faith. It is
rather like the situation where in deciding to go to a particular
destination you decide to take the scenic route and then out
of curiosity follow various side roads until eventually you
are way off course and a long way from your intended goal.
Similarly we need to be aware of being consumed by non-
essential issues which can dominate in church life.

Paul's central aim or God's goal in this passage is that
our faith in Christ will lead to love for others. This needs
to be applied to each of us as it is so easy for our church
communities to fail to be loving and for individuals or
groups to find themselves sidelined. Further, it is easily

possible for us to be so focussed on ourselves that it affects our relationships with non-Christians around us whether at work or in the neighbourhood where we live. Genuine Christianity will be characterised by love towards others.

Proclaiming the message/suggestions for preaching

A preaching outline

Title: **A Church in Danger**

Text: **1 Timothy 1:1-7; 6:20, 21**

1. Beware false teachers at work (1:3, 4a, 7; 6:20)

2. Look where false teaching leads (1:4, 6; 6:21)

3. Steer a straight course to the end (1:4, 5)

Other preaching possibilities:

It would be very simple to leave out the references to 6:20, 21 and to use these closing verses of the epistle for a concluding sermon with similar headings:

+ What was the danger? (6:20):   prizing 'knowledge'

+ Where was it leading? (6:21):   wandering from the faith

+ What must Timothy do? (6:20):   guarding the gospel

The advantage of this is that it can provide a succinct summary to the whole series and draw on other parts of the epistle which link into these key themes.

The other serious possibility is to extend the passage to include the following paragraph which relates to the law so that you deal with 1:1-11. Indeed this may even be the usual course for those wishing to undertake an expository series in 1 Timothy. My reason for not including 1:8-11 in the first sermon is that the time saved may be needed for giving some sort of overview of the letter and for showing reasons why 1 Timothy has particular relevance for the church today. Further, as will be seen in the following exposition, there may well be a virtue in contrasting the law (1:8-11) with the gospel (1:12-17) which may not be quite as apparent if the exposition were to finish at 1:11. Having said this, 1:1-11 is also a natural division – Paul has exposed the false teachers as being teachers of the law (1:7) but then is quick to show that the law itself is good (1:8) and that it does have an ongoing legitimate use (1:9-11).

Leading a Bible Study
Title: **A Church in Danger**
Text: **1 Timothy 1:1-7; 6:20, 21**

1. Introduce the issues

    +   These passages focus on the problems which Paul discerned at Ephesus.

    +   What happens over the course of time if there is no maintenance on a house?

    +   What is likely to happen to the church community if there is similar inattention by the leaders to the needs of the church family?

2. Study the passages

    +   What was the main problem facing the church at Ephesus? (1:3)

    +   What was being taught in the church? (1:3, 4, 7)

    +   What were the results of this teaching which Paul highlights in 1:4,6; 6:20f?

- In what ways would this teaching lead to people wandering from the faith? (1:6; 6:21)

- According to Paul what should be the central aim or goal of the Christian life? (1:4, 5)

- What is the overall message of 1 Timothy bearing in mind the instructions to Timothy at 1:3; 6:20?

3. Think it through

- In what sort of situations is it possible that the contemporary church might fall into these errors?

- How would you know if any of the hallmarks identified at 1:4, 6; 6:20 were evident in our own teaching or behaviour?

- How should Paul's aim in 1:5 affect the way we live as Christians?

- What is the best way to guard the gospel (6:20) in our situation?

4. Live it out

- How can we avoid the dangers highlighted by Paul in this passage?

- How could the central aim of showing love be more evident in our lives?

2. THE GLORIOUS GOSPEL OF GRACE (1:8-20)

Introduction

In this passage we find a clear focus on the glorious gospel of our Lord Jesus Christ. Having identified the false teachers as being also 'teachers of the law' Paul needs to remind Timothy that the law is indeed good but it needs to be used properly (1:8-11). However, the main thrust of the passage is to move from the preaching of the law to sinners to the experience of receiving the gospel of grace, which fills Paul with such wonder that he bursts out in praise to God (1:12-17). Having highlighted that a genuine gospel ministry must focus on the cross of Christ, Paul then resumes his urgent charge to Timothy that in order to resist the false teachers (1:3) he will need to fight the good fight, as indeed Paul had already been doing (1:18-20). Consequently, 1 Timothy 1 holds together as a distinct section within the epistle, beginning and ending with the need to resist the false teachers and their teaching, but with the dominant theme that the church must once again receive the doctrines of grace and keep the cross of Christ central in everything.

Listening to the text

Context, structure and observations

Context

In one sense verses 8-17 are a digression from the key announcement to Timothy, that of being instructed or charged to deal vigorously with the false teachers (1:3, 18 for repetition of 'charge'). However, 1:8 flows out of the reference to the false teachers being teachers of the law, in order to justify the correct handling of the law. It may well be that the legalism and asceticism (1:7; 4:3) which Paul had observed in Ephesus had resulted in an inward-looking church purely focusing on its own internal affairs. If so, then Paul's autobiographical section where he celebrates Christ's grace, mercy and patience (1:12-17) functions as a wake-up call to the church at Ephesus to show them that they had taken their eye off the ball and were no longer functioning as a gospel-centred, outward-looking church seeking to glorify God through the advance of the gospel.

Structure

There are three main paragraphs within this passage and these naturally provide us with a clear structure for understanding Paul's flow of thought. The central section splits into two parallel paths.

A.	1:8-11	What or whom is the law for?
B.	1:12-17	Compare the law with the effect of the gospel!
	1:12-14	Work of Christ ... Paul's sin ... experience of mercy/grace in commissioning
	1:15,16	Work of Christ ... Paul's sin ... experience of mercy/grace in conversion
	1:17	Overflowing of praise to God
C.	1:18-20	What should Timothy do in order to restore this gospel-centred ministry to Ephesus?

Once again being sensitive to the structure and thought-flow of the epistle will shape the way in which the preacher expounds the passage.

Observations

1:9, 10 comprise a list of sins which at some points show a clear correspondence with the Ten Commandments. Commentators vary in how many of these commandments are being referred to, with some limiting it to commandments four to nine whilst others see all ten commands represented. Ultimately, it probably makes little difference to the preaching of this passage.

1:12-16 include a tremendous heightening both of sin and of grace. It is not just that Paul is a sinner. Instead, he piles up the words describing his pre-conversion life (1:13 blasphemer, persecutor, violent man) and twice states for emphasis that he is the worst of sinners (1:15, 16). On the other hand, the passage does not just speak of Christ's mercy but uses an array of different words (mercy, grace, patience) to describe how Christ has treated him. Further, these words are then stretched to their greatest capacity in order to magnify Christ's love (abundant or overflowing grace and unlimited or perfect patience 14, 16). The preacher will want to convey the tone of the passage as much as the content in order that the most natural response of our hearers is identical to that of Paul's at 1:17 in overflowing with praise to God.

Though it may not affect an exposition on this passage it will be useful to note that the encouragement to Timothy to fight the good fight (1:18) is repeated near the end (6:12), which reveals the significance of this instruction and how critical Paul views the situation. Perhaps reference should also be made to the number of times that references to Satan, the devil or demons appear within 1 Timothy (see 1:20; 2:14 by implication; 3:6, 7; 4:1; 5:15). Paul is clear about the spiritual battle that is involved in seeking to restore the gospel to its rightful position in the church at Ephesus. Perhaps it should also be noted that in Paul's experience in planting the church in Ephesus in Acts 19 he encountered much occult activity. All these things serve as indicators of the reality of the spiritual battle as the gospel advances.

Exposition

Utilising the structure already identified, the exposition is based on the three main paragraphs in this passage.

God's law exposes sin (1:8-11)

The natural inference from 1:7 is that if the false teachers were primarily teaching the law, then clearly the law is bad. Paul could not allow such an inference to be drawn and so he immediately counters such thoughts at 1:8 with the statement that the law of God is good if it is used properly. Creation is good (4:4) and the law is good (1:8) but the key point concerns usage.

How were the false teachers using the law? It would appear from what Paul says at 1:9 that rather than use the law to convict outsiders of their sinfulness, these teachers were using it to instruct Christians. However, rather than building Christians up by showing them how the law, rightly interpreted, corresponds to Jesus' two great commands to love God and to love neighbours (Mark 12:30, 31; Gal. 5:13, 14), it was being used to gain knowledge (6:20) that was speculative (1:4 ESV) and which was unapplied to their lives. It had become meaningless talk (1:6) rather than a means by God's grace of transformation.

Historically, Christians have spoken of three uses of the law. First, it is given to convict unbelievers of sin and in this way lead the sinner to Christ. Second, it is given to restrain evil within society. Third, it is given to educate and teach believers, already saved by the grace of the Lord Jesus Christ, in order to shape lives that are pleasing to God. In these ways it can be seen that there is no conflict between the Old and New Testaments since there is a clear ongoing purpose for the law. As we shall see, Paul is primarily concerned in this passage with the first use of the law (1:9) but the third use may be observed at 1:11. Nor indeed is the second use completely absent (see 2:2). All of these uses stand in contrast to the law being taught to Christians merely for head knowledge in such a way that it had no contact with bringing people to Christ or helping Christians to conform to a godly lifestyle.

The law reveals the depth of sin (1:9,10)

A health check in itself does nothing. If something is found to be amiss, it certainly can't make you better without any further medication or intervention. What it does is highlight where something is wrong. Similarly, at either end of Paul's list in 1:9, 10 we find that the law is made or given to reveal to us whatever is contrary to sound (literally this means healthy) doctrine. The teaching of the false teachers had not highlighted sin due to their focus on knowledge, speculation and myths, and as a result the behaviour of the church had become sickly (1:4) and in some cases terminal with people departing from the faith (1:6). By way of contrast, Paul wants the law to be preached to non-Christians in order to expose what is wrong so that the medicine of the gospel can be applied and gladly received.

The law reveals the breadth of sin (1:9, 10)

The list of sins exposed by God's law is not limited in view to one or two issues. Instead it is comprehensive and covers the full range of sin. Tentatively I would agree with the view that Paul is referring to all of the ten commandments in these verses[1]. Rather than go into detail (which may be possible if the preacher is expounding only 1:8-11, rather than a larger passage) it can be seen that the law has an impact in identifying

---

1   George W. Knight *The Pastoral Epistles* (Carlisle, UK: Paternoster, 1992) pp. 84, 85.

behaviour that is viewed by God as sinful across the whole spectrum of life. It may be that some sins are more serious in their consequences than others within the list (lying is not as serious as murder) but each sin reveals the people to be, in the words of the opening phrase in Paul's list, lawbreakers and rebels before God. Though 'the practice of homosexuality' (note: not homosexual orientation in and of itself) is included within the list alongside other sexual sin, namely, adultery, it is clearly not the only sin on Paul's list. Christians will want to note that 1:10; Romans 1:26, 27 and 1 Corinthians 6:9-11 each affirm that the practice of homosexuality is sinful, but they will want to do so recognising that the law also exposes many other practices as wrong.

The law reveals the height of Christian behaviour (1:11)
Paul could have ended his sentence at 1:10. He has already shown that God's law exposes sin, but in this last part of the paragraph he indicates that God's good law equates to sound or healthy doctrine (1:10) which in turn conforms to the glorious gospel of the blessed God (1:11). In other words there is ultimately no contradiction between the standard of behaviour expected in the Old and the New Testaments. A life conforming to the gospel will conform to God's law and this is the foundation for Paul's later teaching on aspects of Christian lifestyle (e.g. faithfulness in marriage 3:2,12; 5:9).

In summary, Paul spends time contrasting the false teachers' wrong use of the law with its correct usage, in such a way as to show that the law exposes sin and reveals a lifestyle that is not in conformity to a life transformed by the gospel. By speaking of the gospel which had been entrusted to him (1:11) Paul is able to make an easy transition into the next part of his argument which will focus on his own experiences of receiving the gospel and how he came to be entrusted with it (1:12-17). This will not only reveal his authority to correct the false teachers but also move things on by showing what the false teachers should have had as their main focus – the cross of Christ and the grace of our Lord Jesus Christ.

Christ's mercy saves sinners (1:12-17)

The reference to the gospel in 1:11 enables Paul to develop this theme in two distinct ways. In showing how the gospel had been entrusted to him, Paul reveals his position as an apostle (1:1) who has the authority to correct and admonish them (as he had already been doing 1:19, 20). Second, he shows how the gospel had changed his life, lifting him from the depths of sin to know the heights of Christ's mercy and love. If some of the false teachers were asking whether Paul had any right to interfere, then 1:12-14 and later 2:7 provide an adequate response and this may be the reason why, surprisingly, Paul speaks first of his appointment to serve Christ (1:12) before writing about being saved by Christ (1:15, 16) though of course the two events did occur together in Acts 9. It may also be that Paul uses this order so that he can move from an account of Christ's salvation and his conversion directly into praise to God (1:17). Against the background of the presence of the false teachers Paul is wanting to point out that the experience of their teaching of the law led only to sterile discussions and arguments between men (1:4, 6) whilst the experience of receiving the word of the gospel leads to worship and praise to God (1:17).

Paul's apostolic ministry is based on Christ's mercy and

overflowing grace (1:12-14)

Three separate but related themes run through this paragraph (and are repeated in a slightly different way at 1:15, 16).

1. Christ's initiative (1:12) – not only did He entrust the gospel to Paul for safekeeping (1:11 and see 6:20 for the need for Timothy to take care of that which has been entrusted to him), but also Christ strengthened Paul and appointed him to his service (1:12). The initiative lay with Christ in calling Paul to this particular role and Paul has been found trustworthy or faithful in this ministry. Whereas the false teachers were presumably self-appointed, Paul can speak of Christ's appointment and perhaps that is why he is keen to stress God's role in the setting apart of Timothy for his ministry of the gospel through words of prophecy at 1:18; 4:14, indicating that neither was Timothy self-appointed.

2. Paul's sin (1:13) – Paul's *curriculum vitae* at the point when he was commissioned did not look particularly promising for a potential church leader as Acts 8 and 9 reveal. He describes himself as a blasphemer, persecutor and a violent man which is all evidenced in his journey to arrest Christians in Damascus. Paul tells it as it is, neither embellishing (he explains he acted in ignorance and unbelief at the time) nor sweeping things under the carpet, in order to magnify God's grace.

3. Christ's overflowing grace (1:14) – Paul's commissioning, given his background, revealed not just God's mercy (1:13) but the overflowing grace of our Lord. Paul paints a wonderful picture of a fountain with water constantly tumbling over the side of the pool as

a glimpse of the amazing grace of our Lord Jesus Christ. No longer was Paul to be characterised by his antipathy to Christ and his church and his violent treatment of his followers, but by faith in Christ and love towards and for others. Such faith and love are signs of a godly life and of Paul being in the centre of Christ's saving purposes, transformed from his earlier life (see 1:4, 5 for faith and love).

On the basis therefore of Christ's sovereign initiative and overflowing grace, Paul has been given apostolic authority by Christ to resist the work of the false teachers.

Paul's personal salvation is based on Christ's mercy and unlimited patience (1:15, 16)
Again we see the three distinct scenes repeated.

1. Christ's initiative (1:15) There are three 'trustworthy sayings' in 1 Timothy and they are to be found at 1:15; 3:1 and 4:9, 10. Presumably this formula is included to give the following words greater weight and significance. This is particularly the case in this first saying, which demands full acceptance: that the reason Christ came into the world was to save sinners. In other words, the purpose of the incarnation was the cross. Again, as at 1:12, it all happened through Christ's initiative rather than due to human planning or at anyone's request. Whereas the teachers of the law were saying that religion was all about how much and what you do, for Paul the gospel was all about what Christ had done. Of course it would be perfectly possible to preach just on 1:15 and indeed it is a wonderful verse from which to explain the glorious gospel. Yet it is when 1:15 is set

within its context of 1 Timothy 1 and the threat from
the false teachers that we more clearly see why Paul has
turned to this particular way of expressing the gospel.

2. Paul's sin (1:15, 16) – Paul has already revealed his
    past (1:13) but now he considers his whole life. He
    sees himself not as having once been the foremost
    of sinners, but as someone who continues to be the
    foremost of sinners. The longer he goes on as a believer
    the more aware he becomes of how sinful he truly is
    and therefore how much he needs the gospel of grace.
    Twice he speaks of himself as the foremost of sinners
    (1:15, 16) to underscore his situation. He is constantly
    recognising that in any league table he lies right at the
    bottom. The false teachers may have spoken of their
    achievements in keeping their rules (4:3) or in the
    acquisition of knowledge (6:20) but Paul cannot speak
    of such things, only of his sin.

3. Christ's unlimited patience (1:16) – Christ's mercy in
    granting forgiveness and eternal life is now explained
    also to be an example of His 'unlimited' patience. Again,
    as with the adjective 'overflowing' in 1:14, it is a word
    that stretches our thinking so that we can see just a little
    bit more clearly how much love for Paul, (and he is an
    example for many others 1:16) lay in Christ's heart.
    Perhaps in our mind we can think of Jesus' famous
    parable of the Prodigal Son and the image of the father
    waiting and waiting … and then running out to meet
    his son when he eventually appeared on the horizon
    (Luke 15:20). The teachers of the law would be able to
    give instant assessments about somebody's obedience
    or knowledge but in the heart of our Lord Jesus Christ

there is a perfect patience, longing and waiting for that
act of repentance and return.

On the basis therefore of Christ's sovereign and saving
initiative, Paul has received new life. This is a gospel that
celebrates Christ's achievement, not man's, and which
promises life rather than meaningless talk, and all due to
the amazing, staggering mercy, grace and patience of the
Lord.

As Paul reflects on his argument which centres on
the importance of God's work of grace and the gospel, in
contrast to the detritus left by the false teachers, he finds
himself unable to go straight on to his call for Timothy
to resist them (1:18). Instead, because Paul had received
overflowing grace and patience (1:14, 16) we now see
him in his own heart overflowing in praise because of the
amazing fact that God, the King, immortal, invisible, the
only God, has accepted him through the gospel of grace and
he bows down and worships with his heart full of praise and
thanksgiving (1:17). The fruit of the ministry of the false
teachers is argument and sterile talking (1:4, 6). The fruit
of the gospel of grace is praise and thanksgiving to God the
King. Similarly any version of evangelicalism which leads
to arguments and controversy must be suspect when set
alongside genuine evangelicalism which delights in Christ,
the cross, overflowing grace and issues in praise to God.

God's church needs protecting (1:18-20)

After the significant 'digression' in 1:8-17 Paul returns to
the presenting issue of what to do about the false teachers.
The charge or instruction is repeated (1:3, 18) to Timothy
that he must resist them because of the significance of the
danger involved if they are steering the ship. This short

passage gives clear guidance concerning how Timothy is to act.

Timothy has received an authoritative teaching role (1:18)
Due to the fact, later acknowledged at 4:12, that Timothy might not have the self-confidence to deal with this problem, Paul reminds him that he has been entrusted with authority from God to act. He receives apostolic affirmation from Paul that he is a genuine believer (my son ... my true son 1:2, 18). Further, he is reminded of God's role in his commissioning to be a minister of the gospel. As 4:14 amplifies, the elders laid their hands on him but this commissioning or ordination was sealed by God's confirming of Timothy to this role via a word of prophecy. In the same way that the apostle Paul was genuinely converted (1:15, 16) and had been appointed by the Lord (1:12-14), so Paul encourages Timothy by reminding him that he has also been genuinely converted and that he has also been appointed by the Lord. Timothy is therefore to exercise his role vis-à-vis the false teachers not in his own authority but with God's authority.

Timothy must fight for the faith (1:18, 19)
As an authentic minister of Christ, Timothy must not ignore the problem at Ephesus. Instead, he is charged with the responsibility of engaging in a spiritual battle – fighting the good fight for the faith (1:18 and see 6:12). Later in the letter he will be reminded that this is to be done in the right manner, for example exhibiting love and gentleness (see 6:11, 12), but for now the most important thing is for Timothy to hold on to faith and a good conscience. In his battle he must not let go of the gospel either personally or in relation to the church. Like a parent holding on to a small child in town, as they cross a busy road, so Timothy is to

consider the faith as precious and something which he must guard (6:20) and hold on to, with every fibre of his being.

Why must Timothy act? (1:19)

Why is the situation so serious that it demands this command from the apostle and this graphic image of warfare? The answer lies in the fact that some of the false teachers have let go of the faith (and see 4:1, 2) and as a result have shipwrecked it. Here lies the danger, that if leaders have shipwrecked their faith, then there is the real possibility that those who follow them may also end up shipwrecked. If the captain of the ship steers on to the rocks the whole crew is affected. Given the seriousness of this danger, with leaders and preachers leading the church astray through their teaching, Timothy must act decisively to prevent further shipwrecks.

What should he do? (1:20)

But what should Timothy do in such a situation? Paul gives an example of what he has already done. He has previously identified two culprits, Hymenaeus and Alexander. Given the likelihood that they would steer the ship on to the rocks of legalism, Paul has cut them loose from the ship/church in order that the ship would be kept safe. He has done this also so that they might recognise how desperate their own position is amongst the rocks and the surf, so that in due course they might seek to re-board the ship in gratitude for the safety it now provides. Handing them over to the sphere of Satan equates to the exercise of church discipline and expulsion from the fellowship, though with a view to their return once they had recognised the error of their ways.

In summary 1:18-20 completes the call of 1:3 for Timothy to deal with the problem of the false teachers and fully engage with the spiritual battle that this would involve.

Standing back we can now see that at every step of his argument in 1:8-20 Paul has been considering the false teachers either directly or indirectly. They have not used God's law properly in their teaching (1:8-11) and as self-appointed leaders (cf 1:12-14) they have neglected to focus on the heart of the Christian faith – the cross of our Lord Jesus Christ and His overflowing grace (cf 1:15, 16) with the outcome that rather than praise to God their teaching resulted in controversy and friction (cf 1:17). As a result, Timothy must take action, holding on to the faith, which would mean holding on to the glorious gospel of grace, which Paul so movingly describes at 1:12-17. Rejecting the overflowing grace and unlimited patience of the Lord Jesus Christ can only lead to personal disaster graphically described as a shipwreck, and so for the sake both of such teachers and indeed on behalf of the whole church, Timothy must now engage in the spiritual battle for the faith (1:18-20).

From text to teaching

Get the message clear

Big idea (theme)
We must hold on to, and be excited by, the glorious gospel of our Lord Jesus Christ.

Big questions (aim)
Preaching or teaching on this passage should answer the following questions:

1. What is the main purpose of the law?

2. What is so amazing about the gospel of our Lord Jesus Christ?

3. Why is it necessary to fight for the faith as a Christian leader?

Engage the hearer

Point of contact

Imagine a beautiful garden, which over the years has been neglected, so that all sorts of weeds have sprung up and completely obscured from view many of the amazing flowers that had originally been planted. Someone addressing the needs of that garden would have to get involved in the hard work of dealing with the weeds and tending the flowers so that they are back on display for all to see, however, they might also need to sack the gardeners responsible for such negligence. This is exactly what Paul does in this passage. He identifies what's wrong in terms of the false teachers' use of the law. He seeks to put the beauty and wonder of the gospel back on display for all to see. Finally, he has already dismissed two of the church leaders for their negligence.

Main illustration

Paul uses several graphic pictures within this paragraph which are designed to capture our imagination. First, he says, 'the grace of our Lord was poured on me abundantly' (1:14 NIV), or, 'the grace of the Lord overflowed for me' (1:14 ESV). It is a picture of water cascading from a fountain and overflowing around the sides. This is how the grace of Jesus Christ is described. It is a picture of excess and of being overwhelmed by the refreshing waters of grace unleashed in the gospel.

Second, there is the picture of warfare (1:18) and the need to engage in hand to hand combat. Rather than ignore the threat or retreat from the battle a picture is given of a fierce struggle for the soul of the church.

Third, Paul uses the idea of shipwreck (1:19) to describe the result of rejecting the faith. It's a powerful, evocative picture of a ship ignoring all the signals from charts or lighthouses and plunging into the rocks with disastrous results. It is an image designed to help us see that these false teachers, though perhaps very persuasive and interesting, were leading both themselves and others on a destructive course to complete disaster. It's an incredibly strong image designed to stir Timothy up to take action rather than ignore what was happening in the church.

Application

God's Word, and in this case particularly God's law, must be used and handled correctly. It is easy to seek to gain biblical knowledge for its own sake but that will not necessarily do any good and it could even bring harm if such knowledge leads to pride and inaction. God's Word is designed to change and transform us and this is particularly the case with God's law. It is meant to expose our sinfulness and drive us to Christ. It is designed to reveal God's character enabling us to see what a God-centred life, pleasing to Him, would look like. Paul speaks elsewhere of the danger of knowledge puffing us up with pride (1 Cor. 8:1) and the antidote is to let God's Word humble us and drive us to Christ where we find grace, forgiveness and, through the Spirit, strength to live a life more pleasing to Christ in conformity to His Word.

Each generation has its blind spots when it comes to recognising what is sinful. From our perspective, it is difficult to understand how those engaged in the slave trade over 200 years ago could not have seen from 1:10 that their actions were wrong. In our day, many of us might immediately recognise the practice of homosexuality as wrong (1:10) and yet at the same time routinely be involved in work practices which amount to lies and deception. Paul's list is designed to show how God's Word exposes every sort of sin and we need to pray that we would be given eyes to see what is pleasing to the Lord and hearts that are willing to submit to Him in repentance and faith.

As a Christian, it is easily possible to become over-familiar with the gospel so that it no longer excites us and causes us to delight in the Lord Jesus Christ. Yet the way that Paul explains things in the autobiographical section (1:12-17) is indeed meant to be an example (1:16) so that we will also be amazed and staggered by the overflowing abundance of the grace of Jesus Christ and His unlimited patience. Any versions of Christianity which fail to excite us about the cross of Christ and which do not lead our hearts inexorably towards worship of God must be suspect.

The gospel message in 1:15 must be applied to all. People need to know why Jesus came into the world and what He did in order to save us, however sinful we might be. There is a simplicity to this message of good news which needs to be preached clearly and boldly so that we, like Paul, are able to rejoice in Christ's mercy, grace and patience. There should be a clear evangelistic thrust to any sermon based on these verses, reminding Christians of the wonder of the gospel but challenging non-Christians about their need for a Saviour and setting forth the Lord Jesus Christ as the means of salvation.

The danger and the results of false teaching need to be exposed through the vivid illustration of shipwreck used by Paul (1:19). It is easy for church leaders to sweep things under the carpet or file in the 'too difficult to handle' tray. But this passage teaches us that when false teaching has taken a grip, some Christian leaders at least must be involved in the spiritual battle (done with gentleness 6:11,12) of holding on to the faith. Such action may not be easy and may not be popular, but if the situation is serious the church leader must be prepared to take appropriate action.

Proclaiming the message/suggestions for preaching

A preaching outline
Title: **The glorious gospel of grace**
Text: **1 Timothy 1:8-20**

+ God's law exposes sin (1:8-11)

+ Christ's mercy saves sinners (1:12-17)

+ God's church needs protecting (1:18-20)

Other preaching possibilities:
Clearly, if it has been decided that it would be easier to handle 1:8-11 alongside 1:1-7 in the opening exposition, then that will leave 1:12-20 as the text. The preacher might want to use 1:11 as the hook for the sermon in the following way:

Intro: Paul has been entrusted with this glorious gospel (1:11)

1. This gospel is glorious (1:12-17) so delight in it!

2. This gospel has been entrusted to us (1:18-20) so hold on to it!

Equally, such is the richness of the material, particularly in 1:12-17, that the preacher might wish to divide it into its three component parts 1:8-11, 12-17 and 18-20. The problem is that the background context of the danger posed by the false teachers might be lost whereas it may be more evident if you are able to link 1:18-20 with the earlier material. However, one might well feel that to do justice to the amazing nature of God's grace in 1:12-17, the preacher is compelled to spend more time in this chapter.

An evangelistic sermon on 1:15 would be a natural possibility. The text is simple and compelling. It could be used at a Christmas evangelistic event or carol service which seeks to answer the question, why did Christ Jesus come into the world? The following brief points could be made:

1. Who is Jesus? (the Christ)

2. What did He do? (come into the world)

3. Why did He do it? (to save sinners)

4. What must I do?

Leading a Bible Study
Title: **The glorious gospel of grace**
Text: **1 Timothy 1:8-20**

1. Introduce the issues

   + What are the precautions which can be made for a ship to avoid a shipwreck? What needs to be done if these precautions are not followed?

2. Study the passage

   + What would amount to a proper use of the law according to Paul? (1:8)

+ What effect should the law have on the people described in 1:9, 10?

+ In what ways does Paul describe himself in 1:12-16 before he encountered Christ?

+ In what ways does he describe how Jesus dealt with him in 1:12-16?

+ Why does Paul include 1:17 in this passage?

+ Why does Paul think it necessary to talk of the need for 'fighting the good fight'? (1:18) What might it involve? (1:19, 20)

3. Think it through

+ Are there any sins within this list which we deem more acceptable, or even not as sinful at all? (1:8-11)

+ How should the clear focus of Christ in 1:15 shape the agenda of the church?

+ In what ways has Christ shown you mercy, grace and patience? (1:12-16)

+ To what extent is it still important for Christian leaders to fight the good fight? (1:18-20)

4. Live it out

+ How can we find ways of keeping our focus on Christ and His amazing grace?

+ How can we enable our churches to avoid a shipwreck in our generation?

Part 3

RESTORING THE CHURCH

1 Timothy 2:1–3:13

1. The glorious gospel is for everyone (2:1-7)

Introduction

The first section of 1 Timothy corresponds to 1:1-20, it begins and ends with Paul's charge (1:3, 18) to Timothy to deal with the false teachers who had appeared in the church at Ephesus. In the midst of these instructions Paul has focussed on his own experience of the gospel and the grace of our Lord Jesus Christ (1:12-16) which stands in contrast to the teaching of these other teachers who focussed on the law (1:7; 4:3) and which had led to various controversies (1:4; 6:3-5).

Within the next main section of 1 Timothy, which runs from 2:1 through to 3:13, Paul is now seeking to instruct Timothy in terms of how he wants to see the church at Ephesus re-shaped, with a renewed focus on the gospel and godly living, as a contrast to the legalism and ungodliness evident in these other ministries. This second main section therefore includes material about the centrality of the gospel (2:1-7) and the vital importance of godliness not only for church members (2:8-15) but also particularly for those engaged in church leadership (3:1-13). The next main marker occurs at 3:14, where Paul once again returns to speaking more directly to Timothy about his own conduct and what is expected of him in this situation, which therefore gives us a strong indication that 2:1 to 3:13 is our next section.

If section one highlighted the presenting problem and was directed particularly to Timothy, section two is now addressing the needs of the church at Ephesus in order to show what a gospel-centred, godly church will look like.

Listening to the text

Context, structure and observations

Context

There are several clues indicating that 2:1 marks the beginning of a new section of the letter. First, Paul repeats the phrase 'I urge' at 2:1 which echoes the same phrase that opened the previous section at 1:3. Second, the word 'then' or 'therefore' appears at 2:1 indicating that this material appears as a consequence of the previous section. Third, Paul uses the phrase 'first of all'. This may simply mean that the matter he now deals with is the first in a list of items, or it may also have the connotation of 'first importance'. Either way, whilst flowing from the previous chapter, Paul is about to embark on a different tack.

Structure

First, it is helpful to look at the structure of the whole section 2:1-3:13. Given that Paul has introduced the picture of the danger of shipwreck one can see what needs to be done. The ship needs to be steered away from the rocks into deeper water. The behaviour of the crew needs to be dealt with and given the fact that two of the officers on the ship have been dismissed (1:20), guidance is needed in the appointment of new leaders to sail it. This is exactly what we find in this section:

A.	2:1-7	the church must be steered into the deep waters of the gospel
B.	2:8-15	the crew must be encouraged in behaviour pleasing to the Lord
C.	3:1-13	new leaders need to be appointed who will faithfully steer the ship

Second, we can discern a clear structure within our current passage which partly links with Paul's fourfold use of the word 'all' (2:1, 2, 4, 6).

A.	2:1, 2	Prayer for all
B.	2:3, 4	God wants all to be saved
C.	2:5, 6	Christ died as a ransom for all
D.	2:7	Preaching to all (the nations/Gentiles)

In contrast to the narrow legalism of the false teaching, which would lead to an inward-looking policy, with elite groups consisting of those superior in obedience or knowledge, Paul wants the church to launch out once again into the wider world in order to share the glorious gospel with its message for all people.

Observations

The term 'God our Saviour' comes several times at 1:1; 2:3
and 4:10 and underlines the significance of the gospel for
the church at Ephesus.

Whereas the teaching of the law led to controversies
and arguments amongst men (1:4; 6:3-5), the gospel of our
Lord Jesus Christ leads not only to praise (1:17) but also to
prayer to God (2:1, 2) and preaching to all (2:7).

Paul is concerned about the way in which the church
functions within society and for its reputation. This is
revealed at 2:2 and also later on e.g. 3:7; 5:7f, 14; 6:1.

Exposition

Using the structure identified above based mainly on the
recurrence of the word 'all', the exposition divides into four
brief, but very important sections, which contrast with the
narrowness and limited vision of the false teachers. Given
the occult and sinful practices of Ephesus, it is in one sense
understandable that some leaders should have constructed
a wall of regulations around them (1:7; 4:3) in order to
provide security and protection. However, one of the
dangers of building such an edifice is that you then only
focus on things within the walls and you become inward-
looking, with a corresponding lack of concern or interest
for those outside. Prayer also then becomes self-centred
and limited in vision. In contrast to all this, Paul's vision is
outward-looking and extensive, as he longs for the gospel to
make an even greater impact on the world around.

Prayer for all … for the advance of the gospel (2:1, 2)

As at 1:3 where Paul 'urged' Timothy to remain at Ephesus,
so Paul now 'urges' the church at Ephesus to make prayer
a top priority. It needs to come top of the agenda for the
church.

How should the church pray?

Paul includes a list of all the different aspects of prayer, which encompasses a variety of different types of request as well as thanksgiving. It is not easy to distinguish the difference in some of the terms, but the sheer variety serves Paul's point by showing that prayer is a rich activity and it helps to underline the importance of the request to be made. A child asking for a particular item, perhaps the latest toy or gadget, first asks, then pleads and seeks to persuade .... and if she receives the item, responds appropriately in thanksgiving. Though it is conjecture, perhaps that is what is going on in this list, indicating the urgency of the requests that the church at Ephesus should be making. They are to ask, plead, keep asking ... and then respond with thanksgiving as God graciously answers.

For whom should the church pray ?

The church is simply to pray for all people (2:1). It will include praying for those on the list who have broken God's law at 1:9, 10. As we shall see, 2:2 is a slight digression in the argument. Connecting 2:1 with 2:3 we can see that praying for all sorts of people is pleasing to God our Saviour. This probably also answers the unspoken question concerning what the church should be praying for. If God is described principally as 'God our Saviour' who has a desire for people to be saved (2:3, 4) then presumably the thing that is particularly pleasing to this God is if His people are praying for all people to be saved. God is pleased when our will, represented in our praying, coincides with His will.

Returning to 2:2, we may ask why Paul needs to include specific encouragement to pray for kings and all those in authority. Surely they are already included in the request to pray for 'all people'? Clearly Paul felt that he needed to add something by way of reinforcement. Perhaps some church leaders might say that there would be little point praying for an ungodly emperor such as Nero who, depending on whether 1 Timothy was written towards the end of the 60s A.D., might well have been on the throne. Further, given Ephesus' occult links and temple worship, both described in Acts 19, perhaps many would have seen it as futile to pray for leaders within such a community. Whether or not this is the case, we need to ask what 2:2 adds to Paul's instructions for the church to pray and why he has inserted it at this point.

1.   Paul views God as the King of Kings

Pray for kings because God is the king (1:17) or as 6:16 asserts 'the king of kings'. God is the sovereign one over all the kings of the earth and therefore there are no 'no go' areas for the Christian when it comes to praying.

2.   Paul is concerned for the reputation of the church

The actions of the false teachers had generated a bad reputation for the church in Ephesus as can be seen at 3:7; 5:7, 8, 14 and 6:1. This would inevitably affect the expansion of the church and so the burden of Paul's letter is that the church would know how to conduct itself in a manner pleasing to God (3:15). The purpose clause within 2:2b indicates that Paul is encouraging the church to pray for the civic leaders, whether Christian or not, so that they will preside over a stable society which will provide the right environment for the church to live a life that would win the respect of outsiders. Interestingly, there is a close parallel between 2:2 and 1 Thessalonians 4:11, 12. In both there is the hope that Christians will lead a quiet life, not stirring up trouble and difficulty. At 1 Thessalonians 4:12 the purpose of such a quiet and productive life is that 'your daily life may win the respect of outsiders'. Primarily 2:2 is a call for prayer for leaders concerning how they rule, but embedded within the verse is the call for Christians to live a life characterised by peace, godliness and holiness. Perhaps there is a parallel with Jeremiah 29:7 – as you pray for the city to prosper so you will also prosper. As Christians then win the respect of outsiders within the community, so the right environment is provided for people to come to a knowledge of the truth (2:3, 4).

What should the church pray for?
Building on the previous point, we can see that as the church engages in prayer for all people, including especially the national and civic rulers, there are at least three topics which are evident.

1. Prayer for civic leaders to act in a way that enables the church to thrive by providing wise and stable government. Rather like a gardener spreading a net over some fruit bushes in order to protect them from birds and to ensure growth and fruitfulness, so the church is to pray for civic leaders to act in such a manner that the church can be protected from certain threats, in order to bear fruit. Just as the gardener's net does not protect against every threat (eg. bad weather or other pests) so praying for stable and civic government does not protect the church from indwelling sin or gusts of false teaching. Nevertheless, it is a wise gardener who protects his crop and it is a wise church that heeds 2:2 and prays for its national and civic leaders.

2. Prayer for church members to live godly lives. Paul's aim throughout the letter is summed up in 2:2 with his desire that church members should live 'peaceful and quiet lives in all godliness and holiness'. Such an aim is good in its own right but also serves to win the respect of outsiders.

3. Prayer for the salvation of everyone. The prayer for all sorts of people in 2:1, 2 is to be seen chiefly in the light of that which especially pleases God our Saviour at 2:3, 4. It is prayer for the gospel to advance throughout society.

So within these verses there is a useful guide concerning what the church in Ephesus should be praying for.

God's love for all is the basis of prayer for all (2:3, 4)
The prayer of 2:1 for all people is securely grounded in the heart of God who has revealed Himself especially as our Saviour (1:1; 2:3: 4:9, 10). The thing that is 'good' in 2:3 is the church praying for all people to be saved, because that is God's very own desire also. When we pray such things we are praying in line with God's own heart. Within 1 Timothy there are frequent references to things that are good. God's law is good (1:8). God's created world is good (4:4). Godly living, demonstrated for example in acts of practical service, is good (5:10) … and prayer for people to come to a knowledge of the truth is good (2:3, 4). These are the things which God delights in and which Christians should also be enthusiastic about.

What does God our Saviour want?
He wants all people to be saved. This is of course the very reason that the Lord Jesus Christ came into the world

(1:15) which was to save sinners. Salvation is the central ingredient in Christ's mission and in God's heart. The question arises, however, whether or not this leads to universalism since, if God is the King, then what He desires must surely happen? There are several responses which can be made. First, it is quite clear, even from 1 Timothy, that not all will be saved. There is a place of judgement (5:24) and a place where people plunge into ruin and destruction, piercing themselves with many griefs (6:9, 10). So Paul cannot be saying that every single person will be saved. Second, it is possible that 'all' refers to all types of people. Whether someone is Jew or Gentile (2:7), or whether they are a ruler (2:2) or a citizen, God welcomes all sorts of people into His Kingdom. Third, we need to recognise that there is a difference between desire and decree. Though God clearly desires that everyone might be saved, nevertheless, at the same time, God Himself knows that this will not happen and even sends His Spirit to indicate that some will abandon the faith (4:1). In other words, some He longs for are also those whom He knows will not ultimately be saved. However, the main clue to interpreting this verse lies, as always, in the context.

Given Paul's other writings in the New Testament on issues such as predestination and election (eg. Rom. 8:28-30; 9:6-24; Eph. 1:3-10) which show that not all will be saved and that this is in accordance with God's plan, perhaps it is not necessary to be so defensive about Paul's terminology in 2:3, 4 (and for that matter at 4:10). Paul's aim in this letter is not to say everything there is to say about God's love. Instead he is wanting to address the specific issue in Ephesus where a narrow vision and an unbiblical legalism have restricted the vision of the church.

In this context, Paul wants to expand the horizons of the church with a clearer vision of the love of God our Saviour. All sinners are welcome to enter through Christ, whatever the sin (1:9, 10). That is why Christ came (1:15). And Paul himself is the example of a great sinner whose salvation through the unlimited patience of Christ stands for all time as an encouragement to any sinners who would wish to receive eternal life (1:16). Whoever you are, whatever you've done, the message is that God is a loving Saviour. This is at the heart of Paul's message as he seeks to get the church at Ephesus back on track with a greater passion and focus on the gospel.

How will the church get back on track?

According to Paul people are saved as they come to a knowledge of the truth (2:4). The truth of salvation must lie at the heart of the church's message in order to enable people to be saved. This has two consequences. First, it means that the church must clearly preach the truth and this is picked up by Paul when he refers to his own ministry at 2:7 ('a teacher of the Gentiles in faith and truth' (esv)). The church must not be distracted by other things from this central task of preaching and teaching, which is why for Paul (2:7), Timothy (4:13) and for the elders at Ephesus (5:17) it is to be their central role. This letter will have much to say about issues such as pastoral care (5:3-16) but preaching the truth is to be the priority because knowledge of the truth is essential.

The second consequence is that it reveals how dangerous different or false doctrines (1:3; 6:3) are for the life and mission of the church. Such teaching is not just unhealthy for church members, but it also prevents non-Christians from coming to a knowledge of the truth. It therefore affects the whole future growth and vitality of the church. Seen in this light, it is no wonder that Paul is so vigorously opposed to such teaching.

Christ's death for all is the basis of God's love for all

The next two verses directly follow from 2:3, 4 and are linked by the connecting word 'for'. These two verses explain which truth people particularly need to know in order to be saved and at the same time provide a basis for the assertion that God's love extends to all. This knowledge is particularly focussed on the person and work of Jesus Christ.

Christ is our mediator (2:5)

Since there is only one God in contrast to the many gods and goddesses found at Ephesus (see Acts 19), how may He be approached and how can people find favour with Him? The answer is that the gulf between God and man is bridged by the God/man Christ Jesus. He has already been referred to at many points within chapter 1 as part of the Godhead, but at this point Paul stresses that He is also a man, precisely so that His role as mediator can be emphasised. He acts as the one way to approach God. One can imagine an island connected to the mainland by only one bridge and that is the only route available for people to reach their destination. In the same way we can only approach God our Saviour who is 'the holy eternal, immortal, invisible, the only God' through the person of Christ Jesus. In his own way Paul is echoing the words of Jesus, 'I am the way, the truth and the life. No one comes to the Father, except through me' (John 14:6). So, any teaching about the way of salvation must focus on the person of Christ.

Christ is our ransom (2:6)

What is it that Christ Jesus did which enables us to have access to the living God? The answer lies in His work on the cross, already referred to implicitly at 1:15. On the cross He died, giving Himself as a ransom payment on behalf of, or in the place of, all people. As sinners (1:9, 10), mankind is caught and ensnared by sin (see 3:7; 6:9) and in order to be freed and forgiven we need to be delivered. This deliverance comes through the payment of a ransom price (though in the text it is not specified to whom it is paid). It is a costly price which has been paid, as can be seen in the fact that it cost the Lord Jesus His life. Yet He voluntarily gave Himself for us. Further, it is specifically a substitutionary payment that is being referred to. The prefix to the word for ransom is 'anti' which means 'in the place of' or 'on behalf of'. In other words, Christ pays the ransom price in His death instead of us, so that we might be delivered. This is the doctrine of substitutionary atonement. This doctrine undergirds the doctrine of salvation because it explains how Jesus is able to act as an effective mediator. Christ died in our place, so that through Him the way between God and man could be opened up.

It is this message, to which the teaching about Christ and the cross testifies, that enables people to come to a knowledge of the truth and receive salvation. Teaching about the person and work of Christ is therefore central to the Christian message. The doctrine of substitutionary atonement is not just one theory amongst many which explain the cross. Instead it undergirds every understanding of the cross and on that basis it needs to be central to our proclamation.

As in the above discussion on 2:3, 4, there is here the issue relating to the word 'all'. Did Christ pay the ransom price for every single person, or for 'all' understood in a different way? Again there is the tension between considering a coherent New Testament theology and looking at the details of a specific text. Taking a wider view of the New Testament teaching about the cross and the elect forces us to look at a number of other texts (e.g. in Ephesians 1 the ones who are redeemed through Christ's blood are the ones chosen in Christ before the creation of the world). However, Paul's aim within 1 Timothy is simply to emphasise the breadth of salvation available in contrast to the narrowness of the vision and teaching of the false teachers. In this context, Paul wants to stress the importance of going out to the world with the free offer of the gospel and therefore he does not qualify what he says, or answer the questions of later theologians.

Paul's proclamation to all is on the basis of Christ's death for all (2:7)

Each part of this passage is carefully linked and flows into the other. The message about Christ's death as a ransom for all, to which testimony in the gospel has been given (2:6), must be proclaimed to all. Paul's appointment has already been referred to at 1:12 but now his specific commission is unpacked. In both instances Paul is seeking to defend himself against the false teachers by seeking to show that he is an authentic apostle. At 2:7 he does this by inserting the parenthesis that he is telling the truth and not lying. But what is his role, how does he do it and to whom does he speak?

What is Paul's role?

Paul describes himself as a herald (or preacher – see 2 Tim. 4:2 for use of the same word in a phrase which is often translated as 'preach the word') announcing an important message. He is also a teacher, which is a word frequently used in this epistle (see 3:2; 4:13; 5:17). Further, he is an apostle (1:1). Though others may not be apostles, in highlighting his role as both preacher and teacher, Paul is pointing to himself not just as an example of salvation (1:16) but also now as an example of the sort of ministry which must flow from a true understanding of the person and work of Christ. Seen in that light, 2:7 is an encouragement for all preachers and teachers to see the focus and emphasis of their work as flowing from the gospel message.

How does Paul fulfil this role?

Within 2:7 the phrase 'the true faith' (NIV) could be translated 'in faith and truth' (ESV). The latter is probably a more accurate translation though both are possible – with the NIV the idea is that the Gentiles are to be taught in the faith which is true (ie the true faith). In the ESV the idea is that the teaching is to be done in faith, that is by trusting God, and in the truth. The ESV translation links in with the context of 2:1-7. The paragraph started by encouraging prayer for all and has referred to God as Saviour and the work of Christ on the cross. Paul's role then is to preach the truth about Christ and His substitutionary atonement and he is to do this in faith that is trusting that the God who is Saviour will answer the prayers of 2:1 and bring people to a knowledge of the truth (2:4). It links in to the clear vision of the apostles in Acts 6:4 who gave themselves to the ministry of prayer and the Word of God, a ministry of trusting God to answer prayer and of teaching the truth of God's Word.

To whom does Paul minister?

His ministry, in line with his specific apostolic commission (Acts 9:15), is to be the apostle to the Gentiles. However, Gentiles can be translated 'nations' and brings with it a sense of the universal remit of his preaching ministry. The gospel message is not to be preached only to a few – certainly not just to the Jews (and were there Christians from a Jewish background involved in the legalism and teaching about food laws referred to at 4:3?). God our Saviour wants all to be saved and Christ died as a ransom for all and so this message must be preached to all peoples.

In summary, we see Paul building up to this vision of the gospel being proclaimed to all peoples. This is the calling of the church and especially its leadership. Yet it all starts in the prayer meeting – praying for all sorts of people to come to faith and be saved, including rulers and civic leaders. Such prayer is not a forlorn hope, since it is based on God's desire for all to be saved. This, in turn, is based on the person and work of Christ – His position as mediator and His substitutionary atonement. And this is the message which must be preached to all nations … in faith, trusting that God will hear the prayers of His people as His truth is proclaimed … which brings the paragraph full circle and back to prayer. The centre of the passage speaks of God's work: the love of God and the work of Christ. Either side, at beginning and end, is our work: prayer and preaching. Paul has steered the ship away from the rocks of false teaching into the deep waters of God's love and Christ's death, and into the wide expanse of the gospel invitation to all peoples.

From text to teaching

Get the message clear

Big idea (theme)
On the basis of God's love and Christ's death we are to pray for and preach to all people.

Big questions (aim)

Preaching or teaching on this passage should answer the following questions:

1. What is the contrast between the teaching of the false teachers and the approach of Paul?

2. What is the basis of the gospel going out to all peoples?

3. What is Paul's great purpose in his ministry?

Engage the hearer

Point of contact

It is easy to get into a rut in our praying, either as individuals or as a church, and so have a very limited vision. We become concerned only for our own needs and grow very inward-looking. Paul, on the other hand, wants us to have a much broader vision in our prayers, by developing a gospel outlook which should shake us out of selfish routines in our praying.

Main illustration

Throughout the exposition we have sought to show how the passage is to be seen in context and especially the danger of shipwreck (1:19). One of the main illustrations is therefore to consider how shipwreck amongst the rocks can be avoided. The answer is to steer away from the rocks and into the safe, deeper waters of the ocean. This is exactly what Paul says is to be first priority of the church (2:1) – launching by prayer into the deep waters of the gospel, based on God's love and Christ's death.

Application

This passage should include a straightforward encouragement for God's people to see prayer as a priority. Far too often personal prayer slips off our agenda through our busyness, or it becomes perfunctory and inward-looking. Similarly, this can happen within the life of the church family. As a result the prayer meeting becomes sparsely attended or may even cease to exist altogether. Preaching on this passage should therefore provide an opportunity to help the church family reconsider its priorities.

Alongside the priority of prayer, this section also encourages the church to take seriously its involvement within its community. We should be praying regularly for our national and civic leaders, not only for their salvation but also for them to provide, under God, the right environment in which the church can thrive and the gospel can expand. Alongside this should be a concern for the reputation of the church family within the community and a desire that our witness would not be compromised by the behaviour of Christians.

Our motivation to pray should come not from any new legalism but from reflection on the love of God and the sacrifice of Christ. As we meditate on the wonder of these things, our praying should be stimulated with a greater desire for God's name to be glorified as others come to know the truth and acknowledge Him as Saviour.

Our understanding of the gospel often needs to be sharpened by the sort of texts we come across here. We are clearly told that there is one God and one mediator. Therefore any way of salvation which does not travel through Christ is immediately suspect. However, though the way to God is limited by people coming only through Christ, the gospel invitation is unlimited since Christ's ransom payment is for all. In some places the tendency is to pluralism (many ways to God) and in other places an extreme exclusionism (only preach to the elect), but 1 Timothy 2:1-7 holds the biblical balance of preaching to all about the unique work of Christ.

The doctrine of substitutionary atonement is often under attack, even from within the church. This passage uses a very simple compound word for ransom, which clearly reveals that the ransom price is a payment on our behalf and in our place. Given that salvation is about coming to a knowledge of the truth (2:4) and consists in preaching the truth (2:7), it is striking that preaching about substitutionary atonement comes between these verses (2:5, 6) to highlight how central a doctrine this is.

The Great Commission to preach the gospel to all nations is not just for Paul but for other church leaders and also for the whole church acting together. This sort of passage forces us to re-examine what we are doing and whether mission locally and globally is on our agenda. Like prayer, evangelism is one of the first things that drops off our agenda both individually and corporately. This passage provides a great opportunity then to sort out priorities for the church and for the church leadership. Are prayer and preaching central? Is the gospel the driving force of all that happens?

Proclaiming the message/suggestions for preaching

A preaching outline

Title: **The glorious gospel is for everyone**
Text: **1 Timothy 2:1-7**

1.   The priority of prayer (2:1, 2)

2.   The centrality of God's love (2:3, 4)

3.   The meaning of Christ's death (2:5, 6)

4.   The urgency of preaching (2:7)

Other preaching possibilities:

Those wishing to travel through 1 Timothy at a faster pace may need to consider preaching 1 Timothy 2 as one unit. The two parts which focus first on the priority of the gospel and then on the importance of godliness are linked by the transitional verse 8, which speaks of godly behaviour (connected with 2:9-15) at the prayer gathering (connecting with 2:1). Although there is a considerable amount of material within this, there is of course a case for looking at larger preaching blocks and it does have the added benefit of once again highlighting Paul's solution for the church at Ephesus, namely, the priority of the gospel and godly living.

1. The priority of the gospel 2:1-7

2. The practice of godliness 2:8-15

Those wishing to preach evangelistically to non-Christians or seeking to teach the essence of the gospel to believers may wish to focus on 1 Timothy 2:5, 6 which provides a short gospel outline. It contains material on God, the need for a mediator, the identity of the mediator and the work of the mediator in dying for us on the cross. An outline using the theme of mediator could be:

1. Why do we need a mediator between us and God?

2. Why is Jesus the only person suited to be our mediator?

3. What has Jesus done to make mediation possible?

Leading a Bible Study

Title: **The glorious gospel is for everyone**

Text: **1 Timothy 2:1-7**

1. Introduce the issues

    +   In what sorts of ways do we often find ourselves to be
        in a rut when we pray?

    +   Are there some things/people we always pray for?

    +   Are there other things/people we never pray for?

2. Study the passage

    +   Why, in the context of 1 Timothy, is it striking that
        Paul wants the Ephesians to pray for all people? (2:1)

    +   What do you think lies behind Paul's reasoning when
        he encourages them to pray for rulers? (2:2)

    +   What are we told about God in these verses and why
        is this significant? (2:3, 4)

    +   Why does Paul stress the 'oneness' of God and the fact
        that there is only one mediator? (2:5, 6)

    +   What is meant by a ransom payment and what is its
        effect? (2:6)

    +   How does Paul view his own ministry and to what
        extent does 2:7 apply to the church as a whole?

3. Think it through

    +   How should this passage challenge the way we pray?
        (2:1, 2)

    +   How should understanding what pleases God shape
        our lives? (2:3, 4)

    +   How should the fact that Christ gave Himself as
        a ransom for us shape our lives? (2:5, 6)

+ In what ways should this passage encourage us to see the gospel preached? (2:7)

4. Live it out

+ How can we pray more faithfully for the gospel to advance?

+ How can we encourage each other to have more of a gospel focus in our lives?

2. Godly Living within the Church Family (2:8–3:1a)

Introduction

Within section two of the epistle (2:1–3:13) Paul turns his attention to the church at Ephesus, having already drawn to Timothy's attention in section one (1:3-20) the problems caused by those teaching different or false doctrines. Section two contains two main thrusts. The church is to re-focus on the gospel through prayer and preaching (2:1-7). It is also to re-focus on godly living, both within the church family (2:8–3:1a) as well as within the church leadership (3:1b-13).

The main emphasis in 1 Timothy 2:8-3:1a concerns instructions designed to produce godly behaviour and may form a contrast with some of the activities of the false teachers. Interestingly, Paul divides his comments between men and women. They are clearly equal and not differentiated at all when Paul speaks of the gospel – all, both men and women, have one mediator who gave Himself as a ransom for both of the sexes. Yet, at the same time as being equal before God, Paul feels constrained to offer different guidelines concerning godly living. They are equal and different. Within this framework, Paul then deals with a particular issue that has arisen at Ephesus concerning whether it was appropriate for women to be involved in a public, authoritative teaching role within the local congregation. His response affirms creation differences between men and women, but is done within the overall context of encouraging godly living.

Listening to the text

Context, structure and observations

Context

This passage lies at the heart of the second main section in 1 Timothy. Paul seeks to challenge the church so that it has a clearer focus on the gospel (2:1-7) and godly living (2:8–3:13). This fits in well with the central thrust of the letter revealed at 3:15. There is a strong connection with what precedes, with 2:8 being used as a transition verse. It belongs with our current passage because of the focus on godly behaviour, but it also contains a clear link to 2:1-7 through its reference to prayer (2:1).

Structure

The structure of this passage can be considered in two ways:

A.   Godly behaviour amongst men (2:8)

B.   Godly behaviour amongst women (2:9–3:1a)

Such a structure is straightforward and it should be noted that the practicalities of godly living for women come at the start and the end of the whole section to women. Propriety (NIV) or self control (ESV) comes twice binding the section together – see 2:9f, 15. For the preacher the imbalance of material makes this way of considering the material slightly more difficult to handle, especially given the significant 'digression' evident at 2:11-15.

An alternative way to consider the passage is as follows:

A.   Encouraging godly behaviour amongst men and women (2:8-10)

B.   Rejoicing creation differences between men and women (2:11–3:1a)

Tackling the passage in this manner recognises that the dominant theme is godly living but also provides an opportunity to tackle the important issue of gender differences when it comes to issues relating to church leadership.

Observations
There is a marked change between 2:1-7 and 2:8–3:1a. In the first passage there is the fourfold repetition of 'all' indicating at the very least both men and women. In the second passage there is a differentiation in the instructions for men and women. It is difficult to escape the conclusion that Paul viewed men and women as equal and different. If this applies to the teaching about godly living (2:8-10), it seems natural for it also to apply in areas relating to leadership (2:11–3:1a).

On two occasions within 1 Timothy it can be seen that the original creation order was being challenged and the false teachers almost certainly lie behind both issues. At 4:3 God's goodness in creation in terms of ordaining marriage and providing all sorts of food was being challenged. In our passage at 2:13 Paul reaches back beyond the fall in order to highlight God's original creation pattern. It may well be that the legalism of the false teachers not only had the effect of obscuring the gospel but also obscured God's goodness in creation.

It needs to be recognised that within a difficult passage, 2:15 has a particular challenge with its reference to salvation. Salvation within 1 Timothy is clearly based on Christ's finished work on the cross (see 1:15; 2:6). Yet the experience of salvation at the end is linked by Paul with a life of godliness and this can be seen both here at 2:15 and also at 4:16. It is comparable to the instruction from Paul at Philippians 2:12 for us to 'continue to work out our salvation' and ties together the twin themes of the gospel and godliness.

Exposition

Using the alternative structure offered above there are two main sections.

Encouraging godly behaviour amongst men and women (2:8-10)
The false teachers had built up a wall around the church to protect it from the surrounding culture through their legalistic teaching (1:7; 4:3). The result was an inward-looking church. Paul has already challenged the church to be outward-looking by adopting a gospel focus (2:1-7). However, the wall had actually failed in its job of protecting Christian behaviour. It had not proved to be watertight against the tide of pagan culture and was powerless against the growth of sinful behaviour inside the wall. In this passage Paul seeks to show the ineffectiveness of the instruction of the false teachers by giving simple, clear advice about Christian behaviour and what he expected from the church at Ephesus.

Men (2:8)

The context is that the teaching of the false teachers had led to controversy (1:4), arguments and heated exchanges (6:3-5). Disputes were resolved in a traditional way with anger spilling out. Against that background Paul's instruction is straightforward. Rather than resolve difficulties by resorting to those methods the men should be seeking to settle things through praying together. The sign of godliness for men would be hands raised in prayer to God, not raised in clenched fists towards one another. As Christians, their hands and indeed their whole bodies need to be viewed as holy, that is set apart for God. The gathered prayer meeting was to be at the centre of Ephesian church life and by taking heed of Paul's guidance at 2:1-7 as well as 2:8 it would become a beacon of gospel-centredness and godly living. The Christian men are to be known not for their physical strength and power, however much admired within their culture, but for their prayerfulness.

Women (2:9, 10)
The context is equally important in considering the instructions to women. Some in the church were saying things they shouldn't (5:13) and some had been deceived by Satan (5:15). To counter these and no doubt other issues Paul encourages women to be known above all for their good works (5:10) and self-control (2:9, 15). Though the culture in Ephesus may have prized ostentatious dress, Paul is far more concerned about other things. He lists modesty, self-control and good works and at the end of the passage speaks of faith, love, holiness and self-control once again (2:15). Like the men, they are set apart (holy) and as a result are to be known for their holiness. The outward appearance is not as significant as the fruit of the Spirit being evident within their lives. There is a clear parallel with this teaching at 1 Peter 3:3, 4. So the Christian women are to be known not for their physical appearance and what they wear, but

for the wearing of godliness and good works. Such good works would certainly include the items mentioned later at 5:10 which lists raising children, caring for believers, assisting any in need etc. . .

To put everything together, Paul is concerned about the effect of false teaching on the behaviour of both men and women in the church. He is also concerned that Christians are no longer distinctive within their culture. But they are both to be holy, set apart for the worship of God and this should be evident in their choices about what to do (the men should pray) and what to wear (the women should put on good works). In identifying different issues for the men and the women, Paul is being sensitive to the differences in creation between men and women. Of course they are equal in God's sight but they face different temptations and challenges, which is why Paul has different instructions for them. The recognition of such differences paves the way for the next part of the passage.

Rejoicing creation differences between men and women (2:11–3:1a)
Again we need to recognise the importance of the context within 1 Timothy. The false teachers had, amongst other things, forbidden marriage (4:3). If marriage was out, then so was child bearing, raising children and many aspects of family life. If these things were forbidden, then what would godly living for many of the Christian women look like in practice? Perhaps it might mean that some women could be involved in church leadership on the same basis as the men and in that way serve Christ? If it were argued that some of these women were being deceived by Satan and were wandering away from the faith (5:15) the natural rejoinder would be to point out that it was also men who were wandering from the faith (see Hymenaeus and Alexander 1:20) and that it was the male false teachers who

were responsible for leading the church into error in the first place! If men could be commissioned to teach (3:1) why not women if they were similarly gifted? If some women at Ephesus happened to be deficient in education then all that would be needed would be encouragement for them to learn from God's Word and then they would also be equipped and available for the full range of ministry opportunities within the church. It would appear to be a compelling case and perhaps had led the church to the appointment of female church leaders or at least to its active consideration. After all, with the dismissal of Hymenaeus and Alexander new leaders were needed and why should they not be female? Certainly, this sort of reconstruction would explain why Paul feels the need to address the issue at some point within this letter.

But why does Paul raise the issue at this point in his letter? The answer is that he addresses the question of women teaching (2:11-14) under the wider category of female godliness (2:9, 10, 15). In his argument he wants to show what godly living looks like in practice and it is within that positive framework that he includes this teaching, which seems to forbid women taking on an authoritative teaching role within the local church. If Paul is judged simply on the basis of 2:12 he appears to be negative and restrictive, but seen within the wider context of the passage, this enables us to understand that his aim is positive and affirming of women.

So how does Paul respond to this situation? Let us proceed through the text and see the logical links in his argument.

Paul encourages women to learn … (2:11)
Paul starts on a positive note which may have been very counter-cultural at the time. Whereas other religions including Judaism had little or no place for female

instruction, Paul wants women to be learning from God's Word. Though some translations speak about women being silent (2:12 NIV), the word that is used in both 2:11 and 2:12 has already been used at 2:2 and for the sake of consistency should be translated in the same way each time. Rather than 'silent', the word speaks of being quiet in contrast to being disruptive and bringing the church into disrepute within the community. Though it is a word applied to women at 2:11, 12 it is in fact clearly applied to both men and women at 2:2. It corresponds closely to a quality such as meekness, which is a fruit of the Spirit demonstrated in the life of Christ and which is also enjoined on both the sexes. Submitting to God's Word, and to those who were faithfully teaching it, is to be done within the framework of learning and growing in obedience to Christ.

... however he refuses to permit women to have an authoritative teaching role within the church (2:12)
Each phrase is of importance in this verse. Where interpretations are vigorously contested, it is important to travel very carefully examining what the text says:

1. 'Do not permit' – could this be a personal view of the apostle which is not meant to bind other churches or Christians in later centuries? This is unlikely since Paul speaks as an apostle (1:1) with apostolic authority. Further, as will be seen at 2:13 Paul links his argument with the pattern of creation which strongly suggests that Paul's teaching here applies to all cultures and through the centuries .

2. 'A woman' – could this be an instruction which is only applicable to wives vis-à-vis their husbands, rather than to women generally since the word for 'man' in

2:12 could be translated as husband? This view could be supported by the fact that Paul's example in 2:13, 14 refers to Adam and his wife, Eve. However, this understanding is unlikely, since Paul has been speaking generally to all women in the preceding verses (2:9, 10) and the same term is used to describe the person in 2:11, 12 so that it is difficult to see how the previous instructions in 2:9, 10 could only apply to wives rather than to all women.

3. 'To teach or to have authority' – how is this consistent with Paul's other teaching? He encourages women to teach other women in Titus 2:3 so clearly he recognises that women are gifted and able to fulfil the teaching role in some situations (and which also means that it isn't any lack of education that caused him to restrict women at 2:12). Further, he recognises that women should exercise authority in certain situations as seen for example at 5:14 where Paul uses the word 'manage' which at other times he uses within the context of church leadership e.g. 3:5. So, if in certain situations women can teach and exercise authority what is he saying at 2:12? The situation is further complicated by the fact that Paul only uses the word for 'have authority' once in his writings. Some would argue that it has the negative sense of 'usurp authority.' If so, this could mean that women should not take on the role of leadership in a domineering way, but if done in an appropriate manner perhaps they could exercise authority. This view is considered in the exhaustive research on the meaning of this Greek word conducted by H. Scott Baldwin[1].

---

1   See *Women in the Church: a fresh analysis of 1 Timothy 2:9-15* edited by Köstenberger, Schreiner and Baldwin (Baker Book House: 1995).

A careful exegesis of 2:12 in that work shows that the normal use of this word within this sort of sentence has a positive meaning, parallelling the word 'teach'. 'Teaching' and 'having authority' are closely linked. Through public teaching at the church meeting (and that seems to be the context revealed in 2:8) authority is being exercised. Paul's prohibition in 2:12 is designed to prevent women taking on an authoritative teaching role over the congregation at Ephesus.

Leaders in the church are those who are involved in preaching and teaching publicly (see the elders 5:17) and in managing the church family (see the overseers 3:5). On the basis of 2:12, Paul argues that these leadership roles should not be filled by women. However, many in the contemporary church feel that this is an arbitrary ruling by the apostle, which should now be set aside. What is the justification for Paul's stance? For that we turn to 2:13.

He supports his argument by a reference to creation (2:13, 14). Paul's argument continues with the word 'for' indicating that these next verses provide justification for his teaching in 2:12. He returns to the beginning, even before the fall in Genesis 3, all the way back to Genesis 2 and creation. At other points in his writings Paul does something similar (e.g. see his argument based on the creation order at 1 Cor. 11 which again relates to women in the church). In doing this Paul wants to root his argument in creation so that it is not received simply as his response to the Ephesian culture at that particular point in time but as teaching that applies for all time. Of course, we understand that cultures change and so the Bible must not be followed woodenly. Whether, for example, braided hair in 2:9 is desirable or not is subject to the whims of fashion, but the underlying principle concerning what is important to God stands for all time. Could it be the case that 2:12 was only to be applied literally in that culture at that time? On the basis of 2:13 the answer must be negative. Paul is earthing 2:12 not in shifting cultural expectations but in the unchanging order of creation. His argument is that Adam was formed first, before Eve (2:13), and that the fall occurred when that ordering was upset by the woman, Eve, being deceived by Satan and leading Adam astray (2:14). 2:14 is not arguing that women are inherently likely to be deceived more than men – if so, why would Paul elsewhere encourage them to teach other women (Titus 2:3)? Rather Paul is simply rehearsing the events of the fall as a way of showing what had happened when male leadership had been abrogated, in order to base his teaching in the order of creation itself.

So how can women fulfil their calling to live a godly life? (2:15, 3:1a)

Once again there are difficulties in this verse. How can a woman be saved through childbearing, especially if we take it that Paul is not referring to physical safety during labour? Basically, there are two main ways of approaching this text. It could somehow point to a reference to the Lord Jesus Christ on the basis that having referred to Genesis 2 in 2:13 and Genesis 3:1-13 in 2:14, he now links Genesis 3:15, 16 and the promise of salvation through Eve's seed with 2:15. So through Eve's childbearing we eventually have the birth of the Messiah through whom salvation is received. However, there are several factors that point against this interpretation. First, the reference in 2:15 is to childbearing and not the birth of a child. Second, though one can understand why interpreters are keen to find a reference to Christ at 2:15, the parallel with 4:16 indicates that Paul is perfectly happy to speak of Christians working out their salvation and therefore there is no compulsion to find a reference to the birth of Christ in this verse. So what is the alternative? On the face of it, it looks as though Paul is saying that the normal way down the ages for women to exercise a godly life pleasing to God is within a family setting, which implies bearing and raising children – as long as these women continue trusting in Jesus, showing love, living a distinctive life and exercising self-control. In other words the call to live a life full of good works, pleasing to God (2:10), can be done within a normal family setting (2:15). In support of this view the following points can be made.

First, good works and raising children are directly connected at 5:10. Second, the word for childbearing is also used at 5:14 and refers to having and raising children with the result that there is no need to see any reference in that word to the birth of Christ in 2:15. Third, it makes sense of the 1 Timothy context. Since false teachers (male!) were forbidding marriage (4:3) this would also mean a virtual end to childbearing. If this teaching had really caught hold, how and in what context could younger women find ways to serve Christ and exhibit a godly life? Some were answering this question by seeking to lead the church family. Paul's response is to re-affirm the goodness of the creation pattern by commending the distinctive ministry of women in bearing children and raising them (2:15; 5:10, 14). They are specifically commended to do what men cannot do and which only they can do. This interpretation makes sense of the passage within its 1 Timothy context.

Obviously there are many responses which can be made. Is this verse saying that women must marry and bear children in order to live a godly life? Of course that cannot be correct since then, as now, there would be single women or those who for whatever reason are unable to have children. Nevertheless, Paul's point still stands; that in general bearing and bringing up children far from being against God's will (see 4:3), is actually a normal and godly way for a saved woman to live. If the false teachers were asked how they knew they were on the path to salvation, their answer would relate to the rules they kept, or to the knowledge that they had acquired. Paul wants the women to have full assurance that they are on the path to salvation if they rejoice in God's creation, which includes marriage, childbirth and childbearing and if they rejoice in God's salvation by continuing in faith and love (the very signs identified by Paul at 1:5 which signify the goal of God's work in us).

As we now stand back from this passage we can see that Paul is pro-learning (2:11) and pro-family (2:15) but the one thing he feels unable to support is women taking on the authoritative teaching role within the church family. How this is to be applied in the twenty-first century still needs to be considered, but the basis for any application must be an understanding of what the passage meant to its original hearers. Even though this may lead to a conclusion which is at variance with much of contemporary culture, unless this preliminary work is thoroughly done, we cannot hope to have any confidence in any other resulting applications of the text.

One final point concerns the phrase 'The saying is trustworthy' found immediately afterwards at 3:1a. The punctuation of the Greek text reveals that the sentence beginning at the start of

2:13 does not conclude until the end of 3:1a which seems to show that this phrase is incorporated into 2:15. Equally, since the other 'trustworthy sayings' deal with issues relating to salvation (see 1:15; 4:9.10) and especially given the fact that this formula can occur after the content (see Titus 3:8) it does at the very least challenge the usual chapter division between chapters 2 and 3. It reinforces the importance of 2:15 in Paul's argument, that it is not to be considered as an addendum but as the central thrust of the passage. indicating how women can normally work out their own salvation. Though 2:15 might appear to some to be a difficult verse Paul is indicating that we can trust its reliability just as much as we can trust the content of 1:15.

In summary, we return to the fact that, despite Paul's universal gospel application in 2:1-7, he recognises that men and women face different issues as they each work out how to live a life set apart for God, dedicated to Him. Resisting the example of the false teachers at 1:4 and 6:3-5, the men are to be characterised by prayer. Resisting the teaching of the false teachers at 4:3, the women are to work out their salvation through a life of good works, which for many will involve marrying and raising a family as they continue to exhibit faith in Christ and love for others. Men and women are fully equal and also different and such teaching is clearly reflected by the apostle Paul in this passage.

From text to teaching

Get the message clear

Big idea (theme)
Men and women are equal and different and these differences need to be acknowledged within church life.

Big questions (aim)

Preaching or teaching on this passage should answer the following questions:

1. What sort of behaviour is God looking for within the church?

2. To what extent should women be involved in leading the local church?

3. How important is creation order to how we are to live as Christians?

Engage the hearer

Point of contact

The move towards women's equality over the last century and a half has been an extremely important development which Christians should warmly support but, recognising that there are obvious biological differences, do we need to recognise that there are other differences too?

Main illustration

The fashion industry is big business these days for both men and women. The important questions seem to be: what should I wear?; will I look good in this? These and many other questions about our clothing and accessories can dominate our conversation and our spending. This Bible passage is also interested in what we should wear though it reaches different conclusions. Godliness will never be out of fashion as far as Christ is concerned.

Application

Consideration needs to be given to a particular temptation for men, which is to sort things out ourselves resorting to brute force or angry words if necessary. The idea of submitting to God in prayer, seeking His wisdom and endeavouring to live a life set apart for Him, though fine in theory, is often not well exhibited. So, often men are conspicuous by their absence from the church prayer meeting and though this may be sometimes due to demands of family, or work pressures, it has to be acknowledged that in many churches it is the men who fail to give prayer the priority that it deserves.

Consideration needs to be given to a particular temptation for women to focus more on external appearance rather than on inner Christlikeness. It is very easy for us to soak in the values of our superficial culture which makes so much of external appearance, brand names, beauty treatments etc. Our temptations look very similar to the ones identified by Paul at Ephesus. Searching questions need to be asked about the time, money and effort expended in this whole area as compared to the areas in which God is far more interested.

How can churches seek to be faithful to the teaching of 2:11-15 within our contemporary culture when there is so much resistance to what the apostle Paul says? Clearly it is important to see what Paul is not saying. Given his encouragement for women to be involved in certain teaching roles at Titus 2:3, 4, it is important for such ministries to be valued and affirmed. In many cases the local church should seriously consider funding, where appropriate, such female teaching roles, showing that 1 Timothy 2:12 is not a blanket ban on all forms of women's ministry and supporting the distinctive ministry which women are called to perform. However, 1 Timothy 2:12 as interpreted does put certain limits on women's ministry within a mixed congregation and it is not always easy to discern exactly where these boundaries are within modern church life. The ordination of women *per se* is not necessarily an issue, as ordination or licensing is simply a means by which the wider church recognises the ministry of a particular person. Such recognised ministry could relate to various types of service within the local church such as those provided by deacons (diaconal ministry) rather than the authoritative preaching role provided by church leaders (presbyteral ministry).

As we shall see in the exposition of 3:1-13, though Paul does not envisage the appointment of female presbyters/overseers/bishops, he is supportive of female diaconal ministries which, depending on the church or denomination, may receive endorsement through some official, public act such as ordination. Rather than status, the issue in terms of applying 1 Timothy 2:12 relates to function. What are the activities which involve an authoritative teaching role within the local church? Some would argue that if there is a senior male minister then it should be possible for women to preach, lead services and preside at communion services, maintaining that they do not have an authoritative role. Others would be more hesitant and point out that since preaching and teaching to the congregation is clearly such an important aspect of church leadership (see 4:13; 5:17) it does fall into the category of an authoritative teaching role. On this view, whilst women should be encouraged to fill all sorts of ministries within the local church (and be salaried where that is appropriate), they should not be involved in preaching to the whole congregation. However, this in turn does not mean that women should not be involved in other aspects of a church gathering. In 1 Corinthians 11:5 Paul envisages women praying and prophesying in the setting of a public meeting, though once again this comes within the context of male headship. Clearly there may well be differences of opinion concerning whether or not a particular function falls into the category of an authoritative teaching role and generosity is required between believers as they seek to apply this to their own church or denominational setting. Whatever the conclusion reached, it is clear that this verse cuts directly against the idea of women exercising the role of presbyter or overseer/bishop.

God's goodness in creation which is highlighted as an issue at 4:3-5 also needs to be recognised and affirmed here, through Paul's use of a reference to Genesis 2 at 2:13. Whilst believers will want to celebrate God's goodness as Saviour (1:1; 2:4) and in the salvation He provides, it must nevertheless not be forgotten that He is the Creator. Our salvation does not overturn creation but is designed to restore and renew God's created world. The very fact that Paul chooses to earth his teaching in creation itself should be a reminder for believers to be grateful for God's goodness in creation and to accept and treasure how He has created the world, and men and women in particular. Denying the differences between men and women is ultimately a denial of God's goodness in creation. It is important therefore that men and women are seen to be equal and different. Though equally created and formed by God the Creator, equally saved by the Word of our Lord Jesus Christ, males and females are different and at particular points this needs to be recognised.

Some thought should also be developed from this passage concerning what a genuinely spiritual life looks like. It is easy to fall into the trap of thinking that spirituality is measured in terms of prayer, church attendance and various spiritual experiences. That may even have been the case back in Ephesus in the first century. However, Paul reveals at 2:15 that for women a genuine spiritual life can involve marriage and bearing children. Paul is particularly practical and down to earth. Whereas some in Ephesus would have said that such things got in the way of their relationship with God, Paul would want to affirm, both then and now, that for many Christian women they are part and parcel of their spiritual engagement with the Lord .... as long as they continue walking in faith and love. Paul is therefore unashamedly pro-family and pro-children. Any spirituality that resists this conclusion must be considered suspect. Often the church has unwittingly promoted a super-spirituality which has lost contact with God's goodness in creation in terms of work, family, leisure, food, creativity etc. so that the genuine Christian is taught to live in a rarefied atmosphere which has lost contact with the world. Whilst we are called to deny the sinful pleasures of the world, creation in itself is good not in itself evil. Nor should it be viewed as hampering our relationship with the Lord. This verse should be seen as an encouragement to many women in the way that it marries together their distinctiveness in creation (bearing children – a role which men cannot perform) and their experience of salvation. Clearly there needs to be sensitivity, recognising that some women are single and cannot bear children, but the principle concerning the relationship between creation and salvation is nevertheless important to maintain.

Proclaiming the message/suggestions for preaching

A preaching outline
Title: **Godly living within the church family**
Text: **1 Timothy 2:8-3:1a**

1. Encouraging godly behaviour amongst men and women (2:8-10)

    *   men (2:8)

    *   women (2:9, 10)

2. Rejoicing in creation differences between men and women (2:11–3:1a)

    *   Paul encourages women to learn … (2:11)

    *   … however he refuses to permit women to have an authoritative teaching role within the church (2:12)

    *   He supports his argument by reference to creation (2:13, 14)

    *   So, how can women fulfil their calling to live a godly life? (2:15; 3:1a)

This passage is rich in content and in the contemporary context is also controversial. It may be therefore that some churches would wish to travel through this material at a slower rate, preaching it in two sections: 2:8-10 and 2:11–3:1a. If so, it is important to note in the second sermon on 2:11–3:1a that Paul is in the middle of encouraging women to live godly lives. It is not primarily therefore about issues of church order but about routes to godliness.

Another way of handling this passage takes us in a different direction and that is to incorporate the following material in 3:1-7. The purpose in doing this would be to highlight that though 2:11-15 restricts women from certain ministries within the local church, 3:1-7 restricts many men from these ministries also! Though the role of overseer is one to aspire to, many Christian men will not be appropriate for such a role due to various factors that are to be explored within the following exposition. This may be useful in order to seek to be more even-handed in looking at the roles of men and women. In this context it is again of interest to see that a commitment to family life evidenced at 3:4, 5 is not a barrier to godliness but, on the contrary, provides helpful evidence as to the godliness of the candidate.

Leading a Bible Study

Leading a Bible study on a controversial passage of Scripture is not easy. Some people manage to express opinions regardless of what the text says, often adopting entrenched positions. Others can feel extremely vulnerable and personally threatened by the views of others. It is easily possible for a study on this passage to provide more heat than light. It is vital therefore that the study should be conducted with humility (listening to God's Word and submitting to what God desires are fundamental) and graciousness (recognising each other's concerns, whilst speaking the truth in love).

Title: **Godly living within the church family**

Text: **1 Timothy 2:8-15**

1. Introduce the issues

   + In what areas of life is it possible to see the church being shaped by the world and its values? What do we need to do in order to resist this trend? In what ways do you think our interpretation of God's Word is shaped by society around us?

2. Study the passage

   + What do you think was the danger facing some of the men at Ephesus? (2:8 and see 1:4; 6:4, 5)

- What do you think was the danger facing some of the women at Ephesus? (2:9, 10 and see 5:10, 13)

- What is Paul wanting to commend in 2:11?

- What is Paul wanting to avoid in 2:12?

- What is the significance of Paul rooting his argument at 2:12 in the creation narrative of Genesis 2 at 2:13?

- How is it best to interpret 2:15 in the light of 4:3; 5:10 and 5:14?

3. Think it through

- Are verses 8-10 directly applicable to us now? What are the principles which stand behind these verses for us?

- How would you seek to define what an 'authoritative teaching' role in the church is?

- If verse 12 indicates that a woman should not serve as an elder/overseer in the local church, what ministries should be open to her?

- How can we uphold marriage and family life more within our church and our culture?

4. Live it out

- How can we encourage each other to live godly lives which please God?

- How can churches encourage men to pray?

- How can we affirm the full equality and dignity of women whilst holding to verses 11-15?

3. Godly Living within the Church Leadership (3:1-13)

Introduction

The focus within section two of the epistle (2:1–3:13), which is written especially to Timothy in order to correct things in the church at Ephesus, is on the priority of the gospel and godliness. Having highlighted the significance of the gospel of our Lord Jesus Christ (2:1-7) he has addressed the issue of godly behaviour within the congregation (2:8-15). In doing so, he has divided his comments between men and women, but has given particular attention to the qualities of self control and godliness (2:9, 10, 15) amongst women. In passing, he has raised the issue of whether women should function as leaders within the local church setting. This provides the link with the next section (3:1-13) which is given over to the appointment of leaders within the church, though it is done with a very strong emphasis on the qualities of godly living which Paul wishes to see, with surprisingly little reference at all to the skills required for the posts specified. In other words, godly living is once more the theme, but this time with reference to the appointed leaders of the church, as opposed to the members.

Again, it is important to remember the context of the letter. The amount of material devoted to issues relating to leaders (see 3:1-13; 4:6-16 and 5:17-25) is primarily because of the crisis facing the church at Ephesus. Some of the leaders are involved in teaching false doctrines (1:3; 6:3) and their behaviour has been distinctly ungodly. Indeed, things had become so serious that Paul had felt constrained to dismiss two leaders, Hymenaeus and Alexander (1:18-20). In such a situation it would be natural for the church to be thinking about whom to find to replace these men and so Paul picks up this aspect at various points within the central part of this letter.

Listening to the text

Context, structure and observations

Context
False teachers had risen probably from within the church at Ephesus as Paul had warned (Acts 20:29, 30) resulting in ungodly behaviour and the dismissal of two of the leaders (1:18-20). The reputation of the church within the community must have been severely damaged by what was happening, especially with the poor behaviour of the leaders (see 6:4, 5). In such a context Paul wishes to see new leaders appointed who would be particularly noted for their godly behaviour.

The passage follows the material on godly living amongst church members (2:8-15), which had included the significant 'digression' relating to the appropriateness of women in leadership positions within the church and as a result there is a natural transition into the focus on leadership in this passage. This passage also leads into the central section of the letter (3:14–4:16) and indeed to the central verse of the letter at 3.15 with its focus on godliness and the gospel. So it is natural for that section to be preceded by material relating to the godly characteristics that need to be found amongst those who have been appointed to the task of preaching and teaching the gospel.

Structure
There is a simple division within the passage as Paul looks at the two groups involved in leading the church: overseers and deacons (and see Phil. 1:1 for these same categories):

1. Overseers (1-7)

2. Deacons (8-13)

Both parts can be subdivided further and this is explored in the exposition. However, also of interest is the fact that there is considerable overlap between the two parts of the passage. For instance, neither overseer nor deacon is to indulge in much wine (3:3, 8). They are both to be sober-minded (3:2, 11). They are to be people worthy of respect (3:2, 8, 11). Within Paul's clear and simple structure we should nonetheless recognise the overlap of qualities which bind the passage together, and indeed link it with the general requirements of godliness mentioned earlier (2:8-10, 15).

Observations
The passage begins with the 'trustworthy saying' which by being included within chapter 3 would appear to serve as an introduction to the rest of the section. Although this may be possible, the fact that it concludes a sentence in the Greek text which begins at 2:13 strongly suggests that it should be considered alongside 2:15. Further, the various 'trustworthy sayings' found within the Pastoral Epistles generally link in to the theme of salvation (eg 1:15; 4:9, 10) which would provide a more natural link with 2:15 rather than with 3:1b. On the point that the formula about the trustworthy saying generally introduces the substance of the saying, this is not invariably the case, as can be seen at Titus 3:8.

It is striking how ordinary the list is. Apart from the requirement that the overseer should have an ability to teach (3:2) none of the other characteristics would necessarily differentiate him from other mature Christian men.

The terms for church leaders within the New Testament and even within Paul's letters are remarkably fluid. Titus 1:5-7 reveals that the overseer (for which 'bishop' is an alternative translation) is also regarded as an elder. Similarly this is the case in Paul's speech to the leaders of the church at Ephesus at Acts 20:17ff. At Acts 20:17 they are termed 'elders' yet at 20:28 they are 'overseers' (and 'shepherds', from where we get our word 'pastor'!). So it is not surprising that those distinguished by their teaching ability are described in one place as overseers (3:2) and in another as elders (5:17). There is either a large overlap between these two positions or in fact, as in Acts 20 or Titus 1, they are identical, but describe different aspects of their role and function. As bishops they provide oversight over the whole congregation and as elders they are marked by their age, maturity and position within the church. Another term is also used within this passage which is translated as 'manager' (see 3:4, 5, 12) or relates to 'directing affairs' (see 5:17). The fact that this word relates to both overseer and elder once again enables us to see that those two terms are probably identical. The word translated here as 'manager' was used very early on to denote those in Christian leadership. For example, at 1 Thessalonians 5:12 it appears and refers to 'those who are over you' in the Lord. It is a fluid word which captures the idea of directing operations whether in the home (3:4; 5:14) or in the church (3:5; 5:17). This particular leadership function is very important and should not be neglected just because we more generally use terms such as bishop or elder, depending upon the denomination.

It should also be recognised that there is a degree of fluidity relating to the term 'deacon' (see 3:8, 12) as it is also the word that is translated 'minister' or 'servant' when referring to Timothy at 4:6. Though we might adopt the traditional understanding of seeing deacons as those who exercise a ministry of practical service as opposed to a ministry of the Word (see the example of the early church in Acts 6:1ff or the division highlighted at 1 Peter 4:11 between those who speak and those who serve) it is a reminder that it is not easy to make very strong assertions concerning precisely what the deacons did.

Exposition

Within the following exposition it will be seen that the passage is first considered in terms of the two main roles of overseer and deacon, conforming to the structure of the section. However, in the second part of the exposition the common characteristics which provide an overlap between these two roles are considered. In this way the passage is considered from two different angles which complement each other. The advantage of considering the second aspect separately is that by this means it is possible to connect with the thought-flow of the letter, which seeks to highlight above all the need of godly church members and now godly church leaders.

Types of leadership

Two main categories are considered: overseers (or bishops) and deacons.

Overseers (Episcopal/Presbyteral Ministry)

<u>Who are they?</u> The overseers are also designated as elders (see Acts 20:17, 28 and Titus 1:5-7) and as such they would be drawn from some of the senior men within the congregation. (The Greek word for an elder in the congregation gives us the word presbyter and presbyteral ministry. The Greek word for the role of an overseer or

bishop provides us with the term episcopal ministry.) As will be considered later, they were certainly not to be new converts (see 3:6), so they would have been not only mature in years but also in Christian experience.

<u>What do they do?</u> The term overseer or bishop points to the role of watching over a church family. Such oversight would be for the spiritual benefit of the church (Acts 20:28) and is exemplified in the role that Timothy is to play (4:16), where he is to watch over his life and doctrine in order to save both himself and his hearers. The idea of oversight is also linked with the word translated either as 'manage' (3:4,5) or 'direct' (5:17). Oversight is exercised in the way in which the church is run. The overseer is not to be remote from the organisation but fulfils a 'hands on' role amongst the believers steering the ship, directing the work of the gospel.

<u>What do they need to fulfil this role?</u> Though the exercise of such leadership clearly demands a number of attributes and skills e.g. the sort of skills needed for running a family (3:4, 5), the distinctive character of the overseer (3:2) and the elder (5:17) is an ability to teach God's Word faithfully. In contrast to the false teachers who did not really know or understand what they were teaching, these overseers were to have an ability to teach the faith. Paul saw himself as an apostle, but also as a preacher and teacher of the true faith (2:7) and it is this that he wants to see as the distinctive work of the overseer. Whereas the women were not to exercise an authoritative teaching ministry within the church (2:12), this is precisely the sort of ministry which the overseers were to focus on. They were to lead from the pulpit through a ministry of the Word.

Why would you want to take on this responsibility? Once again it is helpful to remind ourselves of the context and the presence of the false teachers at Ephesus. Through their behaviour (e.g. 6:4, 5) they had brought the church into disrepute and, unsurprisingly, a hiring and firing mentality had become established (see 5:19-25 Obviously it will!). Given these factors, it would be understandable if the role of overseer became one that few desired. Yet Paul counters this immediately by stating that the desire to be an overseer is literally to do 'a good work' though it is normally translated as 'a noble task'. Using the translation 'a good work' connects with other parts of the letter such as 2:10 and 5:10. Good works which are pleasing to the Lord include practical assistance to people in need, but also include providing spiritual leadership to the congregation. Far from shunning this role Paul is encouraging some men to see it as a means of pleasing the Lord through their behaviour.

Deacons (Diaconal Ministry)

Who are they? There is reference to the deacon at 3:8,12 as well as a reference to those who serve at 3:13. The main point of uncertainty lies in the interpretation of 3:11 which literally refers to 'the women'. Are the people described in this verse the wives of deacons (as in NIV, ESV) or are they deaconesses (as in NIV mgn)? On the one hand, it is quite possible that it is primarily a reference to the wives – this could fit the structure of the immediate passage: having considered the essential requirements for the deacon at 3:8-10, Paul looks into the home life of the deacon first by considering his wife (3:11) and then looking at his own conduct within the home (3:12) before coming to a general conclusion (3:13). However, given that the word in 3:11

simply speaks of 'women' it is not completely certain that it should be translated as 'wives'. Further, Paul is happy to describe Phoebe as a deaconess in Romans 16:1 and so it is quite possible that Paul had in mind female deacons in this verse. Finally, it would be strange for him to express concern about the wives of deacons without any mention of the wives of overseers earlier. For these reasons it may be fairer and more accurate to see these women in 3:11 as those serving in their own right. So both men and women could fulfil the roles of a deacon.

What do they do? Literally a deacon is a servant and at 3:13 is described as the one who serves. Like Timothy at 4:6, they are servants or ministers of Christ Jesus, but they perform their function by serving the church. Within this passage and even within the New Testament this role is largely left undefined. It does not involve a ministry of oversight but, apart from that, it seems to describe all the sorts of practical ministries which were required within the life of the church.

What do they need to fulfil this role? In asking this question, the concern is with the way in which they were to serve. They were to do this through keeping hold of the deep truths of the faith (3:9). In contrast to the false teachers, such as Hymenaeus and Alexander who had not held on to faith and a good conscience (1:19, 20) or like those referred to at 4:1, 2, the deacons were to be the sort of people who could be trusted to hold on to the deep truths of the faith with a clear conscience (3:9). Though they were not people who necessarily had a gift in being able to teach God's Word like the overseers, nevertheless they needed to be the sort of person who could be trusted not 'to drop the ball', spiritually speaking. They were chosen because amongst their other abilities was a knowledge of the truth of the gospel and a determination to hold on to it.

Why would you want to do this? The result of serving well as a deacon is twofold (3:13). First, it provides you with a good standing amongst the church family. It is a role which people should respect even if it might often involve menial tasks or hard work unseen by everyone else within the fellowship. Second, it provides you with greater confidence and assurance in your faith in Christ Jesus. As you faithfully serve others as a deacon you will find that your faith grows and you reap spiritual benefit. The more you give out in humble service, the more you will receive. Due to the presence of the false teachers, leaders in general were probably under a cloud at the church in Ephesus. Paul felt that it was important to provide encouragement for people willing to consider taking on such leadership roles. So at the beginning and end of the this passage, first to overseers (3:1) then to deacons (3:13), Paul highlights the dignity and value of these roles.

So Paul identifies two basic types of leadership – one episcopal/presbyteral and the other diaconal. Both sorts are needed within the local church. Nothing is said about whether these roles are full-time or part-time, voluntary or require ordination and so on. The terminology, especially for the overseer, is fluid and the job descriptions are general. What is most important, however, is the Christian character of the people who fill these roles and it is to this subject that we now turn.

Qualifications for leadership
As mentioned earlier the dominant note in this passage relates to Christian character and behaviour which is partly a response to the ungodly behaviour of the false

teachers (6:4, 5). As there is a significant overlap between the qualities identified in both the overseer and the deacon, it seems appropriate to look at them together. The key thing is that Paul wants to see people in these posts who are clearly living under the Lordship of Christ and who demonstrate this by their godly behaviour. Rather than look at each of these many items separately, they are gathered for convenience under three headings.

How deep? (3:2, 3)

The issue is whether the candidate's obedience to Christ is thorough and deep or superficial and shallow. Is there a stability and maturity about their faith, or, on the other hand, is this person like a volcano which could erupt at any moment? The most basic question to ask is whether this person is under the control of Christ or liable to slip the leash and run off. This is highlighted in a number of key areas:

+ Sex – are this person's sexual desires under control? If married, are they faithful to their wife? (3:2,12) 'The husband of but one wife' could simply mean that they are not to be polygamous, but the phrase has further connotations. It could well mean 'not divorced and remarried' and certainly points to the idea of the importance of faithfulness within marriage.

+ Speech – in contrast to the malicious talk and controversies perpetrated by the false teachers (6:4, 5) those in leadership are to have their speech under control. They are to be temperate, self controlled, not violent and not quarrelsome (3:2, 3, 11) and though some of these words may refer to behaviour beyond that simply of speech, it is clear that this is an important area. Instead they are to be characterised by godliness (3:3 and see 6:11).

+ Alcohol – imbibing too much wine and drink is also marked out as something that needs to be considered (3:3, 8). Total abstinence is not required (see Paul's advice to Timothy at 5:23) but any consumption is to be carried out in moderation, with an eye to the reputation of the church and the gospel.

+ Money – finances are also to be under control. Rather than being a lover of money or pursuing dishonest gain (3:3, 8) just like the false teachers with their understanding that religion could be a means to financial gain (6:5), Paul wants those in leadership to be generous with their money and possessions, for example in terms of hospitality (3:2), and trustworthy in everything (3:11).

Our desires could be viewed illustratively like a pack of dogs. Each one, if released, could inflict damage. The candidate for Christian leadership should be the sort of person where such desires are firmly on the leash under the control of the Lord Jesus Christ.

How wide? (3:4, 5)

The issue here is whether the candidate's faith is evident, not just at church with like-minded believers, but whether it is also to be observed elsewhere, such as in the home. Are there compartments in his life where genuine faith and godliness do not flourish? Is there a divide between the person in public and that same individual in private? Is there transparency in this person's life, or is there clear evidence of hypocrisy? Though there is often a public/private divide in the lives of many of our political leaders, the apostle is looking for integrity across this divide for church leaders. Paul deals with these sorts of concerns by raising the issue of faithfulness to Christ in the home (3:4, 5, 12). He is looking for a consistency between their Christian life in their own household and God's household and this point is emphasised by Paul's use of the same word for 'household' which describes the family home (3:5) and God's church (3:15). If they are unable to lead, manage, direct, care and provide for their own household then it must raise a question mark about their capacity to do the same for God's household. If this person's faith is not respected at all within the family at home, why would their faith be respected within the church family? Perhaps it should also be added that in the ancient world the home would often be the base for working and business life (as well as the place where the church family would gather). Managing one's household could therefore involve skills in leading and organising affairs which would also be particularly helpful in the running of a church community.

One word of caution is perhaps required at this point. Timothy is later encouraged to be diligent so that people could see his progress (4:15). In other words, Paul is not expecting complete perfection from church leaders. How could he, since he acknowledged himself to be the worst of sinners (1:15, 16)? One hundred percent obedience of the overseer's children is not therefore a prerequisite. As parents we cannot make our children believers as this is a sovereign work of God and there are no guarantees that a particular child will turn to Christ. However, a situation where children grow up without any respect at all for the

Christian faith of their parents must be taken seriously into account in any appointment, argues Paul. Consistency and integrity across each part of the Christian's life are required.

How long? (3:6, 7)

Those who have not been Christians for long should not be appointed to Christian leadership. Perhaps on the evidence of 5:22, 24 this was a problem at Ephesus with the leaders making hasty decisions and sinful patterns of behaviour only emerging later. Had this been one of the factors that had precipitated the rise of the false teachers in Ephesus? In response to this danger, the apostle wisely advises against the appointment of recent converts (3:6). They should not be those who are, literally, 'newly planted', precisely because it is not easy at that stage to tell what fruit will grow in their lives. Perhaps Paul uses this agricultural phrase with Jesus' parable of the sower in his mind. Will this new plant bear fruit or not? Paul's particular concern is with the real possibility of the new convert being appointed to leadership and becoming puffed up with pride and their own importance just like the devil who also arrogantly grasped for more and soon fell (see Isa. 14:12-15). In such situations there is the need for testing (3:10) which may often take time, linking into the advice at 5:22 about not being hasty in making appointments.

It may well be that the teaching at 3:7 is also linked into this same theme concerning the need for Christians to have given evidence of growth and maturity. This verse speaks of the need for the overseer to have a good reputation amongst outsiders. Perhaps we can imagine a situation where someone is converted and there are signs in some areas of his life that they have come under the Lordship of Christ. Perhaps he is zealous for the truth and also possesses gifts in teaching the Bible. Perhaps his general speech has been transformed and no longer is there a torrent of malicious talk coming out of his mouth. As a result, the man is soon appointed as an overseer within the church and the believers are grateful for his clear teaching ability. However, at work his colleagues still see his financial greed and his problems in handling drink. Though his reputation as a believer within the church family is good, his reputation amongst outsiders is largely unchanged. In such a situation, if appointed to leadership and still struggling with major sins, he will bring disgrace on himself, the church and the gospel. The devil will rejoice when the reputation of the church suffers in this way. It should also be noticed that 3:7 links with 3:2 in that both sentences start in exactly the same way in the Greek text. Given also that verses 2-6 comprise one sentence in the original we can see that 3:7 is the climax of the passage. Paul wants the church leader to be above reproach (3:2) in order that they would have a good reputation within the community (3:7) so that the progress of the gospel would not be hindered.

Each of these three tests is designed to show whether and to what extent the gospel of our Lord Jesus Christ has really taken root within the candidate considered for leadership. As will be seen when 3:15 is taken into account, it is the godliness of the church family which enables the truth of the gospel to be displayed. Since this is the case it is of particular importance that church leaders play a significant part in that process. As they lead by example in living godly lives, the truth of the gospel will be displayed and will advance. Conversely, if the church leaders are failing to exhibit such godly standards then the whole mission purpose of the church is adversely affected. Paul is passionately concerned about the advance of the gospel and so he is concerned for the godliness of church ministers and leaders and for their reputation within the community. Perhaps that is why Paul ends this section referring particularly to overseers with regard to the specific issue of their reputation, since this is such a vital component in the advance of the gospel. Further, it can be seen that all the way through this passage Paul is repeatedly seeking people who can be respected or who are above reproach (see 3:2, 8, 11). Paul only wants people to be appointed to positions within Christian leadership who are respected within the church family and the community, which is why he highlights these various indicators in this passage.

In conclusion, Paul is not necessarily seeking the appointment of the most gifted believers though clearly their ability to handle the Word of God (3:2) or hold on to the Word of God (3:9) is essential. Instead, he is primarily seeking for mature, godly Christians with the requisite ability. Godly character is the non-negotiable. It was the famous 19th century Scottish minister Murray McCheyne who said: 'My people's greatest need is my personal holiness'. It is a sentiment that comes out of this sort of passage and reaffirms what the apostle is seeking in order to remedy the damage done by the false teachers.

Within this letter there is a tension that needs to be held together. Paul refers to the personal aspiration of the candidate in becoming a church leader (3:1). In addition is the need for congregational approval as they weigh up whether the desired characteristics are to be found in that individual (3:2-7). However, at 1:18 and 4:14 Paul also refers to prophecies relating to Timothy which seem to act as God's confirmation that he should take on a leadership role within God's church. Ideally each of these aspects should come together to provide assurance both to the candidate and the church that they are the right person for the task.

From text to teaching

Get the message clear

Big idea (theme)
Godly leaders are essential in the life of the local church.

Big questions (aim)
Preaching or teaching on this passage should answer the following questions:

1. In what ways do the roles of overseer and deacon differ?

2. What are the main characteristics that should be evaluated in considering the appointment of both overseers and deacons?

3. What are the dangers if this advice is not followed?

Engage the hearer

Point of contact
Leadership scandals can have a serious effect wherever they happen. They can bring down governments, financial institutions and multi-national businesses (e.g. Enron). Given the media focus on leaders, any organisation will know that to a large extent their reputation is bound up with the conduct of their leaders which is seen by the public or brought into the public domain. It is the same in the church. The reputation of the church is inevitably tied, to a certain extent, with the conduct of its leadership. It is not unknown, tragically, for churches to

collapse almost overnight if a leadership scandal within the church is uncovered. This all highlights how serious these issues are.

Main illustration

A horse that is wild or unpredictable can cause great problems. It could throw its rider and cause danger to others nearby. It would certainly be given a wide berth until restrained. By way of contrast, a horse that has been tamed and which responds obediently to the requests of its rider is a wonderful picture of energy harnessed in order to reach its destination. Similarly, the effective Christian leader is one who has come under the authority and control of the Lord Jesus Christ. Far from being restrictive or burdensome, this is the very means of bringing fulfilment and a sense of purpose as Christian leaders serve their Master, the Lord Jesus Christ, and enable His purposes to be worked out through them.

Application

Consideration needs to be given as to how these different roles of overseer and deacon are worked out within the local church. Denominations vary enormously in the terms that are used to describe the different sorts of leaders they have and perhaps this reflects the fluidity of Paul's terminology even within the Pastoral Epistles. However, the basic point is that in each church family there needs to be some (not just one) who exercise a ministry of oversight, directing and teaching. On the basis of 5:17 this could be termed a presbyteral ministry (as noted above 'presbyter' comes from the Greek term for 'elder'). It could also be termed an episcopal ministry since 'episcopal' comes from the Greek term for overseer or bishop, but usage over the centuries has generally reserved this word for oversight over a number of churches. In addition to presbyteral/episcopal ministry which is distinguished by its teaching function, there is the diaconal ministry provided by deacons which encompasses a wide range of other ministries. Whatever the exact form of church government and whichever titles are used, it is perhaps helpful to consider ministries under these two headings for the sake of clarity. As at 1 Peter 4:11, this gives us ministries of the Word and ministries of service (though recognising that there may be some blurring of the edges). Both are essential. At times the church may have forgotten that the distinguishing mark of the overseer/presbyter is an ability to teach God's Word. At other times the church may have neglected the importance of recognising ministries of service as an honoured role within the life of the local church.

Developing this point further, the overseer/presbyter needs to have an ability to teach God's Word. There are many useful things that church leaders can do in terms of pastoral care, administrative efficiency etc. but the church must recognise that the ability to teach God's Word is a non-negotiable. However gifted a pastor may be in other areas, if this gift is missing then the role simply cannot adequately be filled. The ability to teach is more than just a matter of a love for and knowledge of God's Word, though these are important as essential building blocks. There is also the need for the ability to communicate effectively. And further, it is not just any communication gift but the ability to communicate clearly to this particular church family that is required. All these things need to be considered both in selection processes, whether formal or informal, and also in appointments to church leadership positions.

What should local churches be looking for in their leaders and in those whom they are considering to appoint, whether to the presbyterate or the diaconate (or whatever term is used)? Three factors are often considered: competence, character and chemistry. Churches may often give some time to looking at areas of competence and may listen to sermons and consider the person's track record. Issues of chemistry, in terms of whether there is a 'fit' with others in the leadership, are also likely to be discussed. However, according to 1 Timothy 3, it is actually character which should be at least as important as competence. The deal breaker is not just whether the person can preach, but whether his character matches up to the areas highlighted by Paul. So often ministry within a local church is ultimately hampered by the appointment of a youth leader, home group leader or church warden who does not exhibit these qualities.

The corollary of these various points is the importance of the church members praying regularly for all their various leaders. As Paul himself confessed as he considered his own ministry, 'who is sufficient for these things?' (2 Cor. 2:16). The church needs to be praying for the presbyters to communicate God's Word clearly and for all those in serving ministries, whatever they may be, to hold on to the truth of God's Word. They need to pray for the fruit of the Spirit, in terms of love and self control, to be particularly noticeable in their lives. They will need to pray for the families of leaders and for their children to grow up respecting God's Word and those who teach it. They will need to pray for those converted to grow in Christian maturity such that at the right time they would be useful in ministry within the church. They will need to pray for the reputation of their leaders with outsiders so that nothing hinders the advance of the gospel. Paul starts and finishes this letter by praying for God's grace (1:2; 6:21). That is exactly what is required for both church members and, in particular, church leaders.

Proclaiming the message/suggestions for preaching

A preaching outline

Title: **Godly living within the church leadership**

Text: **1 Timothy 3:1-13**

1. Types of church leaders

    a.   overseers (3:1-7):

    • who are they?

    • what do they do?

    • what do they need to fulfil this role?

    • why would you want to do this?

    b.   deacons (3:8-13):

    • who are they?

    • what do they do?

    • what do they need to fulfil this role?

    • why would you want to do this?

2. Qualifications for leadership

    • How deep? (3:2-3)

    • How wide? (3:4, 5)

    • How long? (3:6, 7)

One obvious alternative is to spend longer on this passage and consider overseers (3:1-7) and deacons (3:8-13) separately.

Although there would inevitably be some overlap because of the way Paul repeats the sort of qualities needed, it might provide an opportunity to focus more on the distinctive roles played by those involved in these different ministries.

Another possibility which could be considered is to gather up the passages in 1 Timothy which deal with leadership. One could look at 3:1-13; 4:6-16 and 5:17-25 as a short series in its own right. The danger of doing such a topical series is that verses can be taken out of context. As we have seen, the background of the behaviour of the false teachers found elsewhere in 1 Timothy is an important ingredient in understanding this passage and so such a series should really only be considered after a careful study of the whole epistle. However, the church is always desperately in need of godly, able teachers and preachers and there may well be occasions when it would be enormously helpful to focus on this topic.

Leading a Bible Study
Title: **Godly living within the church leadership**
Text: **1 Timothy 3:1-13**

1. Introduce the issues

    + In any walk of life what do you think makes a good leader?

    + To what extent might this be the same or different within the church?

2. Study the passage

    + Why might Paul need to stress that the office of overseer is a noble task? (3:1)

    + What is the main difference between the offices of overseer and deacon in 3:2, 9?

- What do you think is involved in being 'able to teach'? (3:2)

- What are the common features within the lists of qualities in 3:2-12? Were there any items included which surprised you?

- Why does Paul include references to family life at 3:4, 5, 12?

- What is the danger of appointing someone to church leadership too quickly? (3:6, 7, 10)

- Why is it important for church leaders to have a good reputation with outsiders? (3:7)

3. Think it through

- Why do we tend to value gifts over graces and competence over character?

- What do you think are the main temptations for church leaders these days?

- What is likely to be the best strategy to raise up good leaders for the future?

- Have you found that serving Christ in the church has led to the results referred to at 3:13?

4. Live it out

- Given that many of the items in these lists are applicable to all Christians, to what extent am I under the control of Christ?

- How can we encourage and help our leaders to fulfil their calling?

Part 4
REMINDING TIMOTHY

1 Timothy 3:14–4:16

1. Godliness and the Gospel (3:14–4:5)

Introduction

1 Timothy 3:14 begins a new section of the epistle which stands at the centre of the entire letter. It runs from 3:14 through to 4:16. It is held together by the two references at 3:14 and 4:13 where Paul specifically speaks about his desire to join Timothy in Ephesus, whilst at the same time providing instructions about how Timothy is to act in this interim period. Within this pivotal section, all the major themes of the letter are laid out once again. Paul clearly sets out his aim in writing, which is to promote godly living as a means for the advance of the gospel (3:14-16), to resist the assault of the false teachers (4:1-5) and to encourage Timothy in his leadership through a focus on godly living, a commitment to the truth and a concern for salvation (4:6-16). Timothy himself is to be a model in his own ministry of defending and confirming the gospel (Phil. 1:7).

Whereas the previous section (2:1–3:13) was focussed on the needs of the church family at Ephesus and was written to remind the fellowship of the central importance of the gospel and godly living, both amongst the members and leaders, this central section is much more clearly linked to how Timothy is to act. 'You' need to know how church ministers should conduct themselves (3:15). 'You' need to point out the dangers of the false teaching and the correct response (4:6). 'You' are to set an example in your personal and pastoral ministry (4:12). 'You' are to be diligent, persevere and watch your life and doctrine (4:15,16). The movement so far in the letter is straightforward. Timothy needs to understand the gravity of the situation posed by the presence of the false teachers (1:1-20). He then needs to start addressing how to bring the church back to a renewed focus on the gospel and godly living (2:1–3:13). And now he is charged with setting a clear example in order to lead the church through these difficult days (3:14–4:16). This central section of the letter therefore provides a microcosm of the whole epistle, as Paul explains to Timothy the main things which he is to do.

Listening to the text

Context, structure and observations

Context

The opening verse (3:14) signifies a change of direction within the epistle. From instructions about overseers and deacons Paul is now specifically addressing Timothy and what he needs to do. This new section runs to the end of chapter 4. It can also be seen that the previous verse (3:13) has concluded the previous section. That section, running from 2:1–3:13, sought to re-establish a focus on the gospel (2:1-7) and godly living and leadership (2:8–3:13). Both these two sub-divisions end with a summary which highlights the main issues. The gospel will lead to the preaching of the true faith to the nations (2:7). Godly living and leadership will lead to the provision of great assurance in the faith (3:13).

Structure
The section breaks down into three main parts which can be sub-divided:

1. The central aim of the letter (3:14-16): focus on godly living and the truth.

2. The reason for the letter (4:1-5): the presence of false teachers at Ephesus and the denial of godly living and the truth.

3. The commission to Timothy (4:6-16): an example of focusing on godly living and the truth.

Observations
As already noted, the references to Paul's impending visit to Ephesus at 3:14 and 4:13 bind the section together.

The content of what the false teachers were saying is to be found earlier at 1:3-7 and here at 4:1-5. This latter passage therefore provides important clues concerning what Timothy and the church were facing.

The reference to faith and conscience has come a number of times (1:5, 19; 3:9) and is now found again (4:1, 2). Holding on to the faith and living it out with a clear conscience links into the main theme of the epistle (the gospel and godly living) and it is the polar opposite to abandoning the faith and living with a conscience that has been seared.

As at 2:13-15 there is a reference to the creation account from Genesis 1, 2. When the truth is overturned and obscured, God's goodness in creation is often overlooked and deliberately rejected.

Exposition
Using the structure identified there are two main sections in the passage:

Focus on living to display God's gospel (3:14-16)
Paul intended to visit Ephesus soon (3:14) but he recognised that he could easily be delayed due perhaps to the difficulty of travel in the winter, or to other pressing concerns elsewhere. In this interim period he passes on key instructions to Timothy.

Godliness is essential (3:15a)
Christians must know how to conduct themselves in God's house. Due to the way that 'house' is used both at 3:4, 5 and now at 3:15, it is clear that Paul is not referring to a place but to the people who live in that household. At 3:4, 5 it is translated as 'household' (esv) or 'family' (niv) and at 3:15 it could equally be translated the same way (as in the niv). The idea of God's people as a family also connects with the way relationships within this family are later described at 5:1, 2 and indeed the whole of the following main section (5:1–6:2) is given over to exploring the implications of some of these important church-family relationships.

Paul is concerned then with Christian conduct and Christian relationships. In the same way that people should instinctively know how to conduct themselves, say, at a board meeting at work, compared to relaxing with friends at a café or pub, so Paul wants Timothy to explain to the church what sort of behaviour is expected and acceptable within God's family. The answer is fairly obvious. In contrast to how the false teachers have been conducting themselves within God's household (see 1:3-7; 6:3-5) with references to anger, friction, argument and malicious talk, Paul is wanting to see godly behaviour as the only acceptable conduct (see 1:5; 2:8-10, 15; 3:2ff).

Since the church is God's household, indwelt by the living God, Paul longs for conduct which honours Him. What sort of behaviour would please the living God (3:15) who is also described as the King eternal, immortal, invisible, and the only God (1:17; 6:15, 16)? By speaking of 'the living God' (and see 4:10) Paul heightens awareness amongst the believers of God's presence and reality. To those who might be taking notice of the presence and activity of the false teachers Paul wants to remind them of a far greater reality. Rather than listening to the false teachers, they are to be aware of God's presence and His desires, which should shape their conduct accordingly.

Godliness enables the truth to be displayed (3:15b)
The church of the living God is described as the pillar and foundation of the truth. The truth is a reference to the gospel of our Lord Jesus Christ which sinners need to know in order to be saved (see references to truth at 2:4, 7). In what way however can the church be the pillar and foundation of the truth? Within Paul's other writings it would appear to be the other way round, with the truth being the foundation of the church. For example, at Ephesians 2:19-22 God's household is built on the foundation of apostolic truth and indeed this would be the normal understanding. Once people base their lives on the truth, they take their place within God's household. In what way therefore is it correct or appropriate to speak of the church supporting

the truth? In 3:15b the church is described as a pillar and foundation of the truth. The function of foundations, pillars and buttresses (the words are variously translated in the different versions) is to provide strength and stability for the whole structure so that it remains permanent and visible for all to see and enter. Apparently the enormous temple of Diana at Ephesus had a roof held up by 100 columns or pillars each 18 metres high which enabled the whole edifice to stand as an eloquent illustration of what Paul was describing. Without foundations, pillars and buttresses such vast buildings would collapse.

Paul uses this surprising illustration to highlight the vital role of godly living within God's household as the means of providing strength and visibility to the truth. Without godly living in the church the truth would be discredited and its visibility would fade away from view. Of course truth comes only from God (see 2:3-7) but here he sees a vital role for the church in upholding and displaying the truth within Ephesus. The behaviour and conduct of God's people are to be the means which enables the gospel to be supported and displayed within the community.

Paul is aware throughout the letter of the reputation of the church within the world. Currently the reputation of the church at Ephesus is not good due to the influence of the false teachers and so the community is particularly aware of arguments and controversies (1:4; 6:3-5) as well as a lack of care within the Christian family (5:7, 8) and lazy employees (6:1, 2). Such issues do nothing to point towards the transforming truth of the gospel and actually hinder the work of the gospel. Paul's response is that he wishes to see the church demonstrating godly living in such a way that the truth of the gospel is put back on display for all in Ephesus to see. Viewed in this light, 3:15 functions as the very centre of the epistle. It is the key to understanding why Paul needs to act and what he wants to see happening. Everything else, whether relating to the appointment of church leaders or caring for church members, is to be seen in the light of this verse.

And of course there is no contradiction with Ephesians 2:19-22. Even in 1 Timothy we see that faith in Christ and consequent membership of God's household are based on a knowledge of truth (2:4). This truth must then be preached for others to enter into God's family (2:7). In these ways Paul's teaching in 1 Timothy is in harmony with his teaching elsewhere. However, the main issues that he faces concern the outworking of the Christian faith, which is why he uses this particular phrase. The gospel has brought sinners into the church, God's family. They are now to live different lives in order that the gospel can proceed even further within Ephesus, so that others will also come to a saving knowledge of the truth.

Godliness puts on display the glorious gospel of Jesus Christ (3:16)

'Mystery' in Paul's letters usually refers to a secret that is now revealed. So, in Ephesians 3:4-6, the mystery of Christ is that now it has been revealed that Gentiles as well as Jews can be members together in God's family. Here, the mystery which godly living reveals is 'the truth' (3:15) but it is further expanded in 3:16. As believers live godly lives, so they put on a display for others to see the glorious gospel of Jesus Christ, described here in poetic form. Whereas the Ephesian crowd chanted incessantly, 'great is Artemis of the Ephesians!' (Acts 19:28, 34) pointing to the greatness of their god, Paul speaks of straightforward godly behaviour which will point to the greatness of our Lord Jesus Christ. Indeed the surprise is that whereas we might have said 'Great is the mystery of the gospel...' Paul actually says 'Great is the mystery of godliness....'. He is able to say this because godly living (the glad obedience to the Lord Jesus Christ of those who have been saved through the death of Christ) is the gospel! Though we might hesitate to pen these exact words, Paul is so passionate about the need for Christians to live godly lives that he is prepared to make such a daring statement.

Concerning how to interpret the six lines of the text about Christ, there are several possibilities. Some would read the six lines as being in chronological order starting with the incarnation, then the resurrection (Christ's vindication) and ending with the ascension (taken up in glory). However, this compresses most of the lines of the text into a very short timeframe indeed and one could query whether, during the forty days between the resurrection and ascension, the message of the gospel was preached among the nations and believed in the world. However, if the final phrase 'was taken up in glory' referred to Christ's enthronement in glory (e.g. 2 Thess. 1:10) then that would make a simple chronological progression quite possible. This is the most straightforward way of looking at these six lines. Another possibility raised by commentators is to divide the six lines into two sets of three with the idea that each set of three refers to Christ being exalted. However, this does not look like a natural reading of the text.

Alternatively we could divide the text into three sets of couplets which each reveal a common pattern. Considered in this way, lines 1, 3 and 5 refer to Christ's bodily appearance ... which was seen ... and which was believed in the world.

In other words, Christ really came in bodily form into the world. This is important in terms of affirming the created order which is under threat with the asceticism of the false teachers (4:3) and reveals that there is no conflict between body and soul. Jesus Christ (the man – see 2:5) genuinely came in the flesh and lived and was observed in the world.

Looking at lines 2, 4 and 6 the common factor is that Christ is lifted up for all to see His glory. The resurrection reveals Him being lifted up from the grave and publicly vindicated by the Spirit. The preaching of the gospel among the nations is a lifting up of the name of Christ for all peoples to hear of Him. Being taken up in glory is the ultimate sign and demonstration of being exalted. Taken together the Spirit (line 2), the church (line 4) and the Father (line 6) all have the same aim of lifting up the name of the Lord Jesus Christ. As an illustration, we can imagine a football manager in the World Cup. His team are in the final but at half time it is clear that they are dead and buried. However, a wonderful change occurs in the second half and his team end up as winners. The manager is now vindicated. His name is praised around the football world. And the manager himself leads the players up the steps in the stadium to receive the glorious prize. Though only an illustration, with all its weaknesses, perhaps it helps to connect these three lines together.

Joining the two distinct strands in this verse we discover two themes held together. Just as the heart of the gospel is that Christ came into the world … in order to bring eternal salvation to sinners (1:15) so the heart of the Christian life is to follow Christ in the world through embracing godly living … in order that the glorious gospel is displayed for all to see (3:15, 16). The church is to be earthed in the world like Christ, affirming creation and seeking to please God … in order to enable the name of Christ to be lifted up so that many others might celebrate His victory.

Seen in this way, 3:16 reinforces the teaching of 3:15 with its focus on godly living leading to the gospel being displayed, whilst it also prepares the way for the rebuke to the false teachers at 4:1-5 who were endorsing behaviour that obscured the truth of God's goodness.

Commentators are divided about which of these three interpretations is best to adopt. In the end there may be little to choose between the first and third interpretations. In the first, the movement chronologically is from bodily incarnation to eternal glory and affirms both creation and redemption. In the third interpretation, the same movement is seen in each couplet. Ultimately therefore the theological message ends up being very similar and either fits with the context and the background of the false teaching being spread in Ephesus.

In summary, the message of 3:14-16 is that the behaviour of God's family should be the means of lifting up and displaying the glorious gospel of our Lord Jesus Christ. This links to the strong missionary thrust of 2:1-7 and Paul's passionate concern for the advance of the gospel (which will also be observed at the end of this section at 4:16).

Beware of teaching which obscures God's goodness (4:1-5)
This next passage is directly linked with what precedes in 3:14-16 by the connective word 'now' (ESV), though this is left untranslated in the NIV. Paul now informs Timothy about the danger posed by the false teachers (4:1-3a) and the response which is required (4:3b-5).

What was the problem? (4:1-3a)
The passage obviously refers to the rise of the false teachers at Ephesus. The easiest way to handle these verses is to ask some fairly straightforward questions of the text.

What would happen? (4:1)

The warning is that some would abandon the faith (like Hymenaeus and Alexander who made shipwreck of their faith 1:19, 20). This is a constant concern of Paul's within the letter (see also 1:6; 5:15; 6:10, 21). Though the false teachers are operating within the church they have abandoned their faith in Christ through their focus on the law. By putting their confidence in the law they have transferred their allegiance and effectively 'abandoned ship'.

When will this happen? (4:1)

The Spirit says that false teachers will come 'in later times' or more literally 'in the last times'. Understanding this phrase as 'the last times' is more helpful because the New Testament understands this description to cover the whole period between the first and second comings of our Lord Jesus Christ. Therefore Timothy should not be at all surprised that such things have happened at Ephesus. If the text is pressed to discover where the Spirit said these things, it is possible to turn either to Matthew 24:10 or perhaps more likely Acts 20:29ff where the Spirit spoke through Paul to the Ephesian elders warning them of the rise of false teachers from within their number.

How will it happen? (4:1,2)

This sort of thing occurs because of the work of Satan. In this letter Paul constantly describes the reality of the work of Satan (eg 3:7; 5:15) who is always seeking to derail people from the truth of the gospel. No wonder Timothy is encouraged to fight the good fight (1:18; 6:12) because the spiritual battle is real. However, it is important to discover how Satan works and as usual it is through lies and deception (4:2) as is evident from his work in Genesis 3 in deceiving Eve (see 1 Tim. 2:14). Deceiving spirits at work amongst the false teachers have led to them spreading lies rather than the truth and this has happened because their consciences have been seared, so that they are no longer sensitive to what is the truth of the gospel and what is error. Getting seared by a red hot object can cause considerable damage to nerve endings and lead to a subsequent loss of sensitivity and feeling. In the same way listening to the lies of the devil had made them insensitive to the truth. Again, just as Hymenaeus and Alexander had rejected the faith and what their consciences were saying (1:19, 20), so this pattern is to be observed again and again in church life as teachers listen to the persuasive lies of the devil, as opposed to the truths of the gospel.

What were they teaching? (4:3a)

The false teachers were forbidding people to marry and requiring that certain foods should not be eaten. This was a form of legalism (see 1:7) which was linked to an ascetic view of the world. In this way, the goodness of God in creation was denied. As mentioned earlier, this had a knock-on effect and it removed from many women the opportunity to exercise a godly life within a family setting (2:15). As we shall see it led to some of these women using their time less profitably (see 5:13). It is possible that the false teachers had originated from a Jewish background which may explain their focus on the law and also their adherence to certain food laws. Regardless of their background, the effect was to obscure God's goodness in creation.

Why were they teaching these things?

It may be useful to explore this next question, though it is not answered in the text (and it is important to avoid too much speculation on the basis of 1:4!). It is important not to paint such a black picture of these false teachers that it has the effect of making them completely remote and irrelevant from everyday life today. Two possible overlapping reasons may have been given by them, which are both plausible. First, these rules may have been designed to protect the church from a hostile, ungodly culture. By building a wall made up of rules, perhaps these false teachers were seeking to prevent the contamination of the church from outside. The problem of course is that sin resides within and therefore rules are a flimsy device to encourage holiness. Genuine holiness is encouraged not by the law but by the gospel itself (see 1:4, 5). Second, adherence to these laws may have been a marker to others of genuine holiness. Rather like a higher degree or MBA qualification may mark out someone as particularly intelligent, so these rules may have indicated to others the strength of your faith. Of course such thinking is dangerous, as the effect of acting in this way divides Christian from Christian by creating first and second-class believers. It also divides the Christian from the world around by indicating that the Christian is abnormal in not enjoying the good things in God's world. Finally, it divides the Christian from God as it means that He is not being constantly thanked for the lavish gifts He has poured out on us in creation.

What was the solution? (4:3b-5)

God's creation is good.
What God has created is good (4:3, 4). As before in the discussion about women's ministry, Paul returns to Genesis 1 and 2. Whether false teaching obscures the gospel or creation, there is to be equal concern, because either way it

prevents people from seeing the truth which the church is meant to be upholding and displaying for all to see. In fact, in each of these three verses there is a reference to God's view concerning the things outlawed in verse 3. God created them (4:3), what God created is good (4:4), and these things are made holy by the fact that God's Word refers to them as being created by God (4:5). Paul is affirming the created world.

God's good gifts are to be received with thanksgiving

The correct response is not to reject God's good gifts but to receive them with thanksgiving. Once again in each of these verses Paul underlines the point. Those who believe and know the truth (as opposed to those who believe the lies of the devil) are to view God's creation with thanksgiving (4:3), nothing God created is to be rejected, but since it is good it is to be received with thanksgiving (4:4), and that is to be done in prayer (4:5). Every parent knows what a child should do when he/she receives a good gift on their birthday. Equally Paul knows what we should do as we receive good gifts from God.

Return to God's Word

The final point is that if we go to rules and traditions we will step off in the wrong direction, whereas if we know the truth (4:3) and return to God's Word (4:5) we will find the guidance which we need. God's Word sets things apart as pleasing to Him and therefore it is no surprise that the job of a church leader is to preach and teach His Word clearly.

So here we see Paul countering the false teachers by affirming God's goodness in creation. We must always beware of any version of Christianity that divides up body and soul, earth and heaven, creation and redemption since

God is Creator and Redeemer. Once again we see the value of 3:16 with the emphasis equally placed on the incarnation and the glorification of Christ which brings together the material and the spiritual under the Lordship of Christ.

In summary, Paul has highlighted in this passage Timothy's main task (3:14-16) which is to ensure that the church family know how to conduct themselves in a godly manner so that the truth is displayed. In contrast, he is to be fully aware of the danger posed by the false teachers, the effect of whose teaching is to obscure the truth (4:1-5).

From text to teaching

Get the message clear

Big idea (theme)
Focus on godly living in order to display the gospel and avoid any teaching which obscures God's goodness.

Big questions (aim)
Preaching or teaching on this passage should answer the following questions:

1. In what way does godly living enable the truth of the gospel to be displayed?

2. What are the hallmarks of false teaching?

3. How should believers respond to God's gifts in creation?

Engage the hearer

Point of contact
Imagine that you have decided to have an extension built on your house. You have great plans for a significant and solid structure. However, the builder indicates that there is no need to dig new foundations for the external work and says

that there is no need to worry about removing one of the supporting walls.... I guess it would be time to get another builder because we know how important foundations and supports are for the stability and permanence of any structure.

Main illustration

If invited to Buckingham Palace for an audience with the Queen there would be certain things that you might want to find out in preparation for the occasion. You would certainly want to discover what dress code was expected. You might also want to find out how to address Her Majesty when you are ushered into her presence. Your conduct in every way would be shaped by the occasion and who you were meeting. You would certainly not wish to behave improperly. Given that our audience is with the living God who has rescued us, and takes place in His own household we will surely want to to ensure that our conduct is worthy. The glorious gospel that has saved us and brought us into a relationship with the living God demands the response of godly living.

Application

We need to recognise the truth contained in 3:15 that the church, God's household, is the means of upholding the truth within God's world. Our behaviour as Christians will be a vital component in enabling the truth of the gospel to be displayed in the world. If our behaviour is ungodly then the truth will be viewed far less favourably, whereas if there is an integrity to our lifestyle as Christians that will serve to help the truth and the church to be respected. Of course we won't be sinless, but we need to recognise what sort of conduct is pleasing to the Lord and will gain the respect of those outside the church.

We need to make sure that we don't deliberately or inadvertently add rules and traditions which have the effect of obscuring the truth of God's Word and bringing in a two-tier Christianity. Adding or subtracting from God's Word is always dangerous in the same way that changing the ingredients of a medicine could be fatal. In general, we are more likely to spot the danger when people subtract from God's Word than when extra rules are added, which means that within evangelicalism it is the latter problem which is more dangerous. A two-tier Christianity often emerges in an unspoken way that can nonetheless be real and we need to recognise the damage that it can do within the church from causing divisions with each other, as well as the repercussions which can follow in terms of our relationship with the Lord and the negative effect it can have on the church's witness to the community.

We must respect the place of our conscience in the Christian life. Though our conscience is fallen and is not always a reliable guide, (that only comes from God's Word), nevertheless God has given us our conscience and it is a good gift to enable us to assess whether a course of action is right or not. To act against our conscience therefore is not safe and to do so regularly puts us in the position where we become desensitised to what is really happening.

As Christians we need to deny ourselves and give no room for evil as we correctly battle against sin, the world and the devil. However, at the same time, we need to affirm the good things which God has created and express that in constant thanksgiving. There are many, many blessings which we, along with non-Christians, have received from God's hand which include food, the beauty of the natural world, marriage, family relationships and many other things. Though even good gifts can be abused and become idols, nevertheless the correct response is to be regularly giving thanks to God for all these good gifts. As Christians we should steer away from any legalism or asceticism which somehow puts a division between God as Creator and as Redeemer.

Proclaiming the message/suggestions for preaching

A preaching outline

Title: **Godliness and the gospel**

Text: **1 Timothy 3:14–4:5**

1.   Focus on living to display God's gospel (3:14-16)

   + godliness is essential (3:15a)

   + godliness enables the truth to be displayed (3:15b)

   + godliness puts on display the glorious gospel of Jesus Christ (3:16)

2.   Beware of teaching which obscures God's goodness (4:1-5)

   + What was the problem? (4:1-3a)

   + What was the solution? (4:3b-5)

There are several other preaching possibilities. The most obvious one is to move through this passage more slowly and look at 3:14-16 and 4:1-5 on separate occasions. Given the fact that 3:15 is the key text for the epistle it may well be helpful to linger here.

Another possibility is to look at the various passages about the false teachers which are included in this letter (1:3-7; 4:1-4 and 6:3-5). It may be helpful to do this in order to understand what was happening at Ephesus which occasioned the letter from Paul (see 1:3). Or it might be helpful to look at it in order to warn people about the danger of drifting from the gospel to legalism and the serious effects which flow from such a move theologically, ecclesiologically and morally.

One other possibility is to gather up the various passages within 1 Timothy which speak of 'the church' (understanding it as a reference to the people rather than the building).

1.   A place of order and oversight (3:4, 5)

2.   A place of godly behaviour and conduct (3:15)

3.   A place of supporting and displaying the truth (3:15)

4.   A place of care and provision (5:16)

Leading a Bible Study
Title: **Godliness and the gospel**
Text: **1 Timothy 3:14–4:5**

1.   Introduce the issues:

   ✦   What is the problem when you come across someone who holds particular views which have no impact on their life at all?

2.   Study the passage

   ✦   How would you justify the claim that 3:15 is of central importance in 1 Timothy?

   ✦   In what ways is the church described at 3:15?

   ✦   In what ways is the church the pillar and foundation of the truth? (3:15) How is this compatible with Ephesians 2:19-22?

+ What connection does 3:16 have with 3:15 and 4:1-5?

+ Why does the sort of false teaching described in 4:3 gain a foothold in the church from time to time?

+ What is Paul's response to such false teaching as described in 4:3-5?

3. Think it through

+ To what extent do we reserve different behaviour for 'church' as compared to the home or at work? (3:15)

+ What examples of godly behaviour have you seen which make the truth of the gospel more favourably received within a community? (3:15)

+ Where are the areas where we might be tempted to reject God's creation?

+ How evident is it that we are thankful to God for His good gifts in creation?

4. Live it out

+ How can we encourage each other to live godly lives within God's household?

+ How can we encourage each other not to separate creation and redemption in the way we live?

2. Godliness and the church (4:6-16)

Introduction

It has already been noted that 3:14-4:16 holds together as one section through the recognition at 3:14 and 4:13 that Paul is seeking to join Timothy at Ephesus. In this interim period before he arrives, instructions are given to Timothy in terms of what he needs to do within the church (3:14-16) and with regard to the false teachers (4:1-5) but the rest of the material within this section is specific direction to Timothy concerning his own ministry (4:6-16). Personal guidance is offered all the way through: 'if you point these things out to the brothers you will be a good minister of Christ Jesus', 'don't let anyone look down on you', 'you will save both yourself and your hearers' (4:6, 12, 16). This is therefore the most intimate passage within the whole epistle in terms of Paul's relationship with Timothy in which he sets out the way Timothy is to lead, by example, demonstrating godliness and a concern for the gospel. Given the importance of appointing leaders to the church at Ephesus, and the amount of space devoted to this subject at 3:1-7 and 5:17-25, Paul wants Timothy to stand as a 'worked example' for the church, so that they can see how leadership is to be carried out in practice. Here is the essence of the epistle – it is to Timothy, but for the church.

Listening to the text

Context, structure and observations

Context

The passage begins by stating, 'if you point out these things ...'. Though some commentators argue that this refers to all that Paul has written up to that point, it seems more natural to see a link only to 4:1-5 or, at most, 3:14–4:5. Either way, Timothy's role is partly to point out the errors of the false teachers, but also to lead the church, by good example and through faithful teaching, in the right direction.

This passage brings to completion the central section of the letter. It began by Paul giving instruction about the importance of good conduct within God's household (3:15) and concludes with Timothy being held up as an example of what that should look like. When we arrive at 5:1, 2, Paul continues to address Timothy directly, it no longer relates only to himself and for this and other reasons it will be argued that 5:1, 2 belongs to the following section.

Structure
The repetition of 'these things' (4:6, 11, 15) indicates that there are three main parts within this passage, giving rise to the following outline:

1. The personal life of a good minister of Christ Jesus (4:6-10) … doctrine and life.

2. The public life of a good minister of Christ Jesus (4:11-14) … life and doctrine.

3. The goal and purpose of a good minister of Christ Jesus (4:15, 16).

This structure has the advantage of working with these verbal clues but one drawback is that it may play down the significance of the 'trustworthy saying' at 4:9, 10. Noticing that issues relating to salvation occur at both 4:9, 10 and 4:16 gives an indication that 'salvation' is the true goal and that this shapes the structure of the passage in the following way.

1. The personal life of a good minister of Christ Jesus (4:6-10).

    • Doctrine – 4:6, 7a – feeding on God's Word

    • Life – 4:7b, 8 – growing in godliness

    • Salvation – 4:9, 10 – focusing on salvation

2. The public life of a good minister of Christ Jesus (4:11-16)

   + Life – 4:11, 12 – setting an example to God's people

   + Doctrine – 4:13, 14 – preaching God's Word

   + Salvation – 4:15, 16 – keep your focus on the goal of salvation

Perhaps there is little to choose between these alternatives but, given the significance of the gospel for Paul in 1 Timothy, it seems more appropriate to work with the second structure.

Observations

There are several phrases and words which occur elsewhere within 1 Timothy and which helpfully tie this passage into the rest of the epistle. The most notable are the following:

   + Timothy is to be learning from God's Word as opposed to the godless myths which were circulating amongst the false teachers (see 1:4 and 4:7).

   + There is reference to God both as Saviour (see 1:1; 2:4 and 4:10) and as the living God (see 3:15 and 4:10 but also 1:17 and 6:16).

   + There is a 'trustworthy saying' at 4:9, 10 in addition to the ones at 1:15 and 2:13-3:1a. Each of these sayings appears to link into the theme of salvation (which is one of the arguments for thinking that 3:1a belongs with 2:15). There is a further link between 2:15 and 4:16 in that both verses speak of salvation, though in slightly unusual ways, giving emphasis to a human role within the process of salvation. The most natural parallels are with passages such as Phil. 2:12

with the command for believers to work out their salvation and 1 Corinthians 9:24-27 where Paul, in an autobiographical section, speaks of running in such a way that he is not disqualified from the prize. Linking 4:10 and 4:16 in this passage, it can be seen that salvation originates from God but believers must keep walking in the route mapped out for salvation.

Exposition

This exposition is based on the second proposed structure referred to earlier and also on the summary verse at the end of the passage (4:16). Timothy is to watch his life and teaching which will lead to the enjoyment of final salvation for both him and his hearers. There are therefore three aspects to consider in both parts of the passage: a godly life, sound learning/teaching and final salvation. Focusing on these things, both in private (4:6-10) and public (4:11-14) will enable Timothy to be viewed as a good servant or minister of Christ Jesus. God's world is good (4:4), God's Word is good (4:6b) and God's servant is good (4:6a) if he watches his life and doctrine clearly.

The personal life of a good minister of Christ Jesus (4:6-10)

Doctrine – 4:6,7a – feeding on God's Word
Timothy is reminded that his public teaching ministry, which involves correcting the false teachers and the effects of their teaching, will only be sustained by his own spiritual diet. There are two features to this diet which Paul particularly highlights:

Timothy must continue to nourish himself on good teaching (4:6).
The only reason Timothy is now in a position to exercise this public ministry is because of the spiritual nourishment which

he has received over the years from God's Word. The word which is translated 'brought up' (NIV) or 'trained' is more literally 'nourished'. As a child grows to maturity through being brought up on a healthy, nourishing diet, so Timothy has grown to maturity as a Christian leader through being nourished on 'the words of the faith and of the good doctrine' (ESV). This needs to be a continuing part of his spiritual life as he feeds on the words of the faith regularly, chewing away in order to gain every benefit from this spiritual food.

Timothy must avoid feeding on false teaching (4:7a)
Equally, Timothy must avoid the equivalent of junk food which, far from building you up, will cause all sorts of health problems when consumed in any quantity. This junk food derives from the false teacher (1:4) and consists of godless myths and old wives' tales. It is difficult to pin down exactly what is meant by Paul in this phrase. They are myths and therefore unconnected to 'the words of the faith' (4:6). They are likely to be stories, anecdotes and traditions passed down which no doubt have the appearance of being of spiritual benefit but which are in fact without any sufficient grounding in God's Word.

In order to carry out a faithful public ministry, Timothy therefore needs to watch his spiritual intake, avoiding the junk food on offer from the false teachers, however popular they may be within the church family (see for example 5:13) and making sure that he continues to feed regularly on God's Word. Feeding on 'good doctrine' (ESV) will help to build someone up into being a 'good minister of Christ Jesus'. Learning regularly from God's Word will enable Timothy to distinguish truth from error and enable him to conduct his public ministry faithfully.

Life – 4:7b, 8 – growing in godliness

It may at first sight be a surprise that the false teaching is not only to be countered by sound or healthy teaching (this 'good doctrine' of 4:6 is the sound or healthy doctrine referred to at 1:10) but also by godly living. According to Paul this aspect is vital as he sees no divide between life and doctrine or between life in private or in public. Godly living will be the natural outworking of a life shaped by God's Word, demonstrating the truth of God's Word. The Scottish pastor Murray McCheyne maintained that it was not great gifts in a pastor but great Christ-likeness that was most important and this is evident from the stress on godliness and leading by example in these verses (4:7, 8, 12).

How is this to happen? Paul says that Timothy is to train himself in godliness. He uses the comparison of physical training. That may be of some benefit (and perhaps there may be a recognition that believers should recognise their own bodies as good parts of God's creation in contrast to the ascetic views of some of the false teachers at 4:3, 4) but the more important benefit comes from training in godliness which yields dividends both now and in eternity (4:8). Physical training is all about developing and strengthening particular muscles in order to be in good physical condition and often requires hard work and regular exercise in order to see significant progress. Similarly, Timothy is to work regularly at developing godly attitudes such as those listed at 4:12 and 6:11 so that he also can see spiritual progress in his life (and as will be seen, it is progress not perfection which Paul is looking for in this passage – see 4:15). Rather than being the equivalent of a couch potato slumped in front of the television, Timothy is urged to be diligent at becoming more loving, more godly, gentler, purer and so on.

Paul confronts the danger of Timothy coasting along, doing nothing to grow in godliness, because the church needs to see the right sort of behaviour worked out in front of them, in the lives of their leaders (3:15).

Focusing on salvation 4:9,10
The 'trustworthy saying' comes at the end of this small section following on from reference to 'life to come'. Once again the trustworthy saying has salvation as its focus. Two aspects are given by Paul, that correspond to our role and God's role:

1. Our role 4:10a
As at Philippians 2:12 Christians are to be involved in working out their salvation and so, as at Philippians 3:12ff, believers are involved in straining for the finishing line, pressing on towards the goal of full and final salvation. For this the believer must labour and strive. If Paul still has only Timothy in mind, then it is of interest to note that he also refers to the labour or hard work of preaching and teaching later on (see 5:17). In other words, in his personal preparation for his public ministry Timothy is to be involved in working hard through his sermon preparation and in other ways in order to enable many others to experience the life to come. Even if 4:10 does not have such a narrow focus, it links with the hard work of training oneself in godliness so as not to miss out on the prize (and see 2 Tim. 4:7).

2. God's role 4:10b
As believers put their hope or confidence in the Lord, so they are given the assurance that they will be saved, whatever their failures in the past. He is the living God who is able to hear our cry and answer prayer. He is the Saviour of all who come to Him, which is obviously the case for believers who have put their trust in Him. The connecting word

('especially') appears strange, but the same construction is used at 5:8 and 17. It seems to denote the chief category in view and it is designed to show where the emphasis falls – believers can have full assurance of being saved. However, it is possible that the word translated 'especially' could be rendered as 'that is' or 'namely' in which case it is a means of clarifying the category which Paul has in mind - the living God is the Saviour of all, *that is* of all who believe. Perhaps this construction is used so that Paul can emphasise the universal appeal of the gospel, as he did as 2:3-6, as against the narrow vision of the false teachers. Either way believers can have complete confidence that God will save them at the end and grant them life in the coming age.

In conclusion, Paul is encouraging Timothy to keep nourishing himself from God's Word. He is to train himself in godliness and as he does these things, which will involve hard work and application, he can be confident that God will save him at the end.

The public life of a good minister of Christ Jesus (4:11-16).

Life – 4:11, 12 – setting an example to God's people
Timothy is to command and teach these things (4:11) by setting the right example himself. He can only teach about the need to maintain a spiritually nourishing diet if he is doing it to himself. He can only encourage others to grow in godliness if others can see that this is something that Timothy is also seeking to do. So Paul now moves the focus from Timothy's personal life to his public ministry. Given Timothy's age – perhaps he is at this point still in his thirties – Paul recognises that Timothy might be looked down upon by some of the senior figures in the church and consequently his teaching might be ignored.

In such a situation it is not good for Timothy to pull rank or produce qualifications. Rather, he should seek above all to set an example in godliness to the believers which will commend his ministry to them.

Specifically, Timothy is to set an example in the areas of speech, life, love, faith and purity (4:12). Two points should be made about this list. First, it echoes some of the essential qualities sought in the overseers (see 3:2-5). Just as the overseers need to have their speech and relationships under control, so it should be for Timothy. Second, the list highlights some of the main areas where the false teachers were failing. In their speech they could be abusive and malicious (see 6:4, 5). With regard to 'life' they denied God's good gifts (see 4:3). In their relationships, rather than demonstrating love they were stirring up controversies (see 1:4). In relation to the faith, it had in some cases been abandoned (see 4:1). In regard to purity, the fact that Paul needs to refer to this at both 5:2 and 5:22 may suggest that standards have slipped. Paul's list is a call for Timothy to set an example to the church through embracing the sort of godly life one would want in church leaders whilst, at the same time, it is a call for him in his behaviour to distance himself from the false teachers.

Doctrine – 4:13, 14 – preaching God's Word.
In this interim period, before Paul returns, Timothy is to be involved in a public ministry of the Word. This is a ministry of reading God's Word clearly (in a context where many would not have the scriptures), preaching it passionately and teaching it faithfully. It is a call to a Bible-based ministry which is securely rooted in God's Word at every point, in contrast to the myths and anecdotes of the false teachers (see 4:7). This gift that Timothy has been given (see 4:14),

which in context presumably refers to his ability to teach God's Word (4:13) is not to be neglected, because he has been set apart by God specifically for this role. There may be a reference here to something which would now correspond to an ordination which can be pieced together from looking at 1:18, 4:14 and 5:22. The church had commissioned him through the laying on of hands by the elders. God had set him apart through equipping Timothy with this gift of teaching, which had been confirmed by a prophetic word. Paul recalls this event in order that Timothy will be encouraged not to neglect this gift but rather devote himself to this ministry. For Timothy to devote himself in this way would mean that he must certainly make this ministry of the Word a priority in his public ministry. Though there may be others things to do, Timothy must not be distracted.

Focusing on salvation (4:15, 16).
As at 4:9, 10, this small section ends with a reference to salvation. The goal of Timothy's ministry is to enable both himself and his hearers to receive salvation at the end. Everything must be focussed on this task and on this destination, to which God will bring them (see 4:10). But how can Timothy be involved in achieving this? As in his own personal life, where he was told to labour and strive (see 4:10), so here Timothy is encouraged to work out his salvation for the benefit of himself and others.

He is to be diligent in these matters, referring both to setting an example in godliness, as well as in his preaching and teaching ministry. This diligence will be seen by giving himself wholly (NIV) or immersing himself (ESV) in these aspects of ministry. If he gives himself wholly to this task then it means that there must be other tasks which he cannot and must not do. And as he practises (ESV) these things the people around should see progress even if not perfection. They should see Timothy perhaps learning to be more gracious in difficult confrontational situations, or perhaps showing more endurance and a greater willingness to fight the good fight (see 6:11, 12). They should see Timothy's teaching ministry develop as he keeps studying hard and seeks to communicate better with the church family. Timothy will never be sinless and there will always be room for improvement in his preaching, but people will be encouraged as they see his progress over the months and years. Rather than Timothy drifting along with the tide and the currents around him at Ephesus, he is to make definite progress as he sets his course for the destination in view. Above all he is to keep watch over his life and doctrine. He is to keep a careful eye on whether things are slipping either morally or in his preaching. Just as the Ephesian elders were expected to 'keep watch over yourselves and all the flock of which the Holy Spirit has made you overseers' (Acts 20:28), so Timothy is to persevere and work hard in this same area. Each of the verses in this passage reveals the way in which Paul is urging Timothy on in his life and ministry. Be diligent … give yourself wholly … watch … persevere. There is a mounting sense of climax as Paul goes through this list until he comes to the end and we can see why there is so much urgency in his tone. It's all because he longs that Timothy and this church at Ephesus will not be shipwrecked (see 1:18-20) or abandon the faith (see 4:1) but will continue safely to their final destination.

In conclusion, this whole passage features an urgent call from Paul to Timothy to lead the church in such a way that the whole church family reaches its final glorious destination. Imagine leading a group of walkers up to the summit of a high mountain. As the leader you will need to be reasonably well nourished and possess a good level of personal fitness in order to get to the summit yourself. At the same time, as the leader of the group you will need to lead by example as well by giving clear directions from the map at every turn in the path. As you do all this, watching out for stragglers, checking weather conditions and personal needs, there will be steady progress until together you reach the summit with glorious views all around. Such is the commission from Paul to Timothy. He will not be in a position to lead unless he is well nourished on God's Word and growing in godliness. His task with the church is to set an example of godly living and give clear directions through devoting himself to the preaching of God's Word. And as he keeps watch over everything so he, under God, will bring his hearers to the experience of full salvation.

From text to teaching

Get the message clear

Big idea (theme)
To be a good minister of Christ Jesus you will need a commitment to godly living and a reliance on God's Word in order to lead people to glory.

Big questions (aim)
Preaching or teaching on this passage should answer the following questions:

1. How important is it for church leaders to be seeking to grow in godliness?

2. How important is it for church leaders to be devoted to God's Word?

3. What should be the aim of being a minister of Christ Jesus?

Engage the hearer

Point of contact

Churches are always looking for leaders for all sorts of important posts within the fellowship such as home group leaders and Sunday School teachers. From time to time they also need to select a new minister. In these sorts of situations, but especially concerning those to be in overall leadership of the fellowship, what are the main things that you should be looking for? What are the sorts of things that you would want to see?

Main illustration

When an Olympic athlete has successfully been awarded the gold medal it is good to reflect on what has happened over the years to bring them to that point in their career. No doubt a healthy diet was important, with many foods being rejected because of the effect they might have had on the athlete's body. Further, there would have been a strict training regime perhaps including very early starts along with discipline and perseverance. Then of course the athlete would need to perform well on the day, keeping a clear focus on what they needed to do in order to break their personal best and achieve a great result at the end. All of these different ingredients which make an Olympic champion need to be seen in the life of a good minister of Christ Jesus in order that an even more amazing result be achieved.

Application

In these various points of application, the most natural thing is to see how this passage should shape the overall leader of the church family. However, to a certain extent, these points should also apply to other leaders within the fellowship. Even if someone does not have a preaching role, for example, the lessons concerning being nourished on God's Word will have a wider application. Perhaps this should be kept in mind as we seek to draw out lessons from this passage.

Those in any form of Christian service must ensure that they are regularly feeding on a healthy diet of sound teaching from God's Word. In the rush and busyness of life with all its demands and pressures it is very easy for this to be squeezed out of our schedules. Equally, it is all too possible for us to be distracted by great stories of what may have happened elsewhere, so that these stories, with their tales of what God has done, become far more exciting than God's Word. Either way, whether through busyness or distraction, if the net effect is that we are failing to be nourished daily on the Word of God, we will soon discover that our spiritual life becomes stunted and our Christian experience arid. In contrast to no food or junk food, we are to feast at the banquet of God's Word so that we are well nourished for service for the Lord Jesus Christ.

It is very easy to coast along in the Christian life and reach a plateau of godliness. We know that our life has been changed by Christ and there is some evidence of the fruit of the Spirit. However, we have now come to the point where we simply accept where we have reached and others around have to cope with our irritability, impatience or pride. Against this background, Paul encourages us to make progress in our struggle with sin and to train ourselves in the practice of godly living. Physical training often involves repetition and serious work to achieve results. How much

more should we, as those seeking to serve the Lord Jesus
Christ, work seriously with the Spirit's assistance to make
spiritual progress over our besetting sins in order that we
don't remain on our plateau.

It is so important to keep the destination of the journey
in view. It provides the purpose and reason for the journey.
Those serving the Lord Jesus Christ need to remind
themselves that their service is not an end in itself. Rather,
the destination is that we and those committed to us, in our
church, home group or children's group, should experience
full salvation when the Lord Jesus Christ returns. Our
destination is to see the glory of the Lord Jesus Christ in
a new earth and new heavens and our aim is to bring many
others with us. Keeping this clear aim will provide focus for
our service and urgency in the task.

In public, every minister will be setting an example to
their flock by the way in which they live their lives and
conduct their ministry. The only question is whether it is
a good or a poor example. Either way, the example set will
speak as loudly as the Word spoken. It is vital that every
minister recognises this factor; otherwise many, for all
their gifts, will labour in vain. Humility and recognising
one's weaknesses is essential, as is a desire for holiness and
a constant pursuit of godliness.

There are many, many demands on the life of a church
leader. They can so easily be swamped by committees,
administrative labyrinths and pastoral complications, each
of which demands a commitment in time and energy. Often
this work will need to be done so that the church is run
efficiently and people are cared for lovingly, but the pastor
cannot do all these things by himself. Recognising the need
for many others to be involved in all sorts of ways, he is to

devote himself to his core business which is to preach and teach God's Word. Pastors will often need to take stock of what is happening within their ministry as, over time, it is deceptively easy for other things to accumulate in the diary.

Pastors are to keep watch over the flock (see Acts 20:28) but also over themselves (see 4:16). It is sad to see people in ministry getting stale and for their preaching to become dull and predictable. Many have found regular attendance and participation at conferences designed to sharpen up preachers and their preaching, such as those run by the Proclamation Trust, particularly helpful. Others find small-scale preaching groups very helpful, where perhaps four ministers meet together once a month or on a quarterly basis, in order for each to preach a sermon that is soon to be delivered. With plenty of opportunity for constructive feedback from supportive friends this can be exactly the sort of ongoing encouragement that many need to keep themselves attentive to the scriptures and devoted to the task of teaching God's Word.

Proclaiming the message/suggestions for preaching

A preaching outline

Title: **Godliness and the gospel: a vision for leaders**

Text: **1 Timothy 4:6-16**

1. The personal life of a good minister of Christ Jesus (4:6-10)

    *   doctrine – 4:6, 7a – feeding on God's Word

    *   life – 4:7b, 8 – growing in godliness

    *   salvation – 4:9, 10 – focusing on salvation

2.   The public life of a good minister of Christ Jesus (4:11-16)

   ✦   life – 4:11, 12 – setting an example to God's people

   ✦   doctrine – 4:13, 14 – preaching God's Word

   ✦   salvation – 4:15, 16 – focusing on salvation

Other preaching possibilities would include dividing this exposition into two three-part sermons based on the structure of the passage.

Sermon 1:   The personal life of a minister of the gospel (4:6-10)

Sermon 2:   The public life of a minister of the gospel (4:11-16)

It may be that this could even be further expanded by including a separate sermon on 4:15, 16 which may be particularly helpful for someone teaching a group of potential leaders or young ministers.

Another possibility would be to use the trustworthy saying at 4:9, 10 as an evangelistic sermon, perhaps at Easter:

1.   He is the living God – the reality of God

2.   He is the Saviour – the saving work of the cross

3.   Put your trust in Him – the response required

Like the trustworthy saying at 1:15 these are clear, succinct summaries which lend themselves to a 'one off' situation.

Leading a Bible Study
Title: **Godliness and the gospel: a vision for leaders**
Text: **1 Timothy 4:6-16**

1. Introduce the issues

    *   What are the difficulties in any walk of life in maintaining your priorities? What do you think might be the particular issues that church leaders could face in this area?

2. Study the passage

    *   What is the essential diet of a good servant of Christ Jesus? (4:6, 7)

    *   Why is training in godliness of such value? (4:7, 8)

    *   Why does Paul include this trustworthy saying at this point in the passage? (4:9, 10)

    *   In what ways does the list in 4:12 reflect some of the qualities in 3:2ff and to what extent does it provide a contrast with the behaviour of the false teachers at Ephesus?

    *   Why is Paul so keen to ensure the priority of teaching God's Word within the life of a church leader? (4:13, 14)

    *   What is Paul looking for in 4:15, 16 and why is it important?

3. Think it through

    *   How can we ensure that church leaders have their souls properly nourished?

    *   What would a ministry seeking to reflect the priorities of 4:13 look like in practice?

* How can we enable and support our church leaders in fulfilling 4:15, 16?

* To what extent should some of the instructions within this passage apply to all believers?

4. Live it out

* How can we encourage each other and especially our church leaders to make the progress referred to at 4:15?

* What aspects of your belief and behaviour do you especially need to watch out for at present?

Part 5

Restoring the Church
1 Timothy 5:1–6:2

1. Godly living with the Church family: caring for those in need (5:1-16)

Introduction

The central section of the epistle (3:14-4:16) has closed on the climactic note of Timothy's role in salvation. Although Paul continues to instruct Timothy directly in the following verses (which have caused some commentators to include 5:1–6:2 within the previous section), this material relates to matters within the church family at Ephesus as opposed to matters relating specifically to the conduct of Timothy's own ministry. There is a transition at 5:1, 2 which links direct instruction to Timothy concerning his own behaviour whilst also setting up the agenda for the rest of the section down to 6:2. Clearly, before Paul returns to the overriding problem of the presence of the false teachers, which will dominate the final section (6:3-21), there were further matters at Ephesus that needed to be resolved which all related to relationships within the church family.

Listening to the text

Context, structure and observations

Context

The dominant positive note within the letter has been the call for conduct appropriate to God's household (3:15), which is the call for godliness. Timothy himself is to exemplify what Paul is looking for in his own behaviour (see 4:7, 12, 15). At this point, Paul now looks more specifically at the church at Ephesus and develops the theme of the church as a family, which has already been highlighted at 3:4, 5, 15. The family image is now outlined (5:1, 2) before being developed in three separate areas. So older men are not to be rebuked harshly and this is linked to the teaching about how the church family should relate to elders (literally a variant of 'older men') at 5:17-25. Older women are to be treated as mothers and this leads Paul to deal with the issue of widows at 5:3-16. Finally, younger men are to be treated as brothers and it is this brotherly relationship which receives attention in the master/slave relationship which concludes the section at 6:1, 2. It is the vision of the church as a family which is the basis for all this teaching. It all flows out of the central appeal at 3:15 which called on believers to conduct themselves as those living within God's household, God's family.

Structure

This section is very clearly structured through the use of two devices. First, as mentioned, the material all relates to relationships within the church family with 5:1, 2 acting as the agenda. Second, each of the sub-sections begins with the call for the members of the church to honour or respect a particular category of people. Though the word is variously translated in our versions it appears at 5:3 ('proper recognition'

NIV; 'honour' ESV), 5:17 ('double honour' NIV, ESV) and twice at 6:1, 2 ('respect' NIV; 'honour', 'not disrespectful' ESV). So the structure of the section is as follows:

5:1, 2   The church as a family with family relationships

5:3-16   Honouring older women ... as mothers (the widows)

5:17-25   Honouring older men ... as fathers (the elders)

6:1, 2   Honouring younger men ... as brothers (the masters)

No specific point is developed concerning how to treat younger women as sisters in absolute purity, though there is a reference to purity at 5:12 echoing its appearance in relation to Timothy at 4:12.

There is also a structure within the first main subsection 5:3-16:

5:3 – introduction – honouring widows ... but who should do this?

1.   5:4-8 the widow's own family should provide:

        A. Care by the widow's own family 5:4

          B. The widow in real need 5:5

          B. The widow not in real need 5:6

        A. Care by the widow's own family 5:7,8

2.   5:9-15 if no family, the church family should provide:

   ♦ those to be included on the list for provision 5:9,10

   ♦ those not to be included on the list for provision 5:11-15

5:16 – conclusion – families should look after their widows, but if there is no family it is the church family who should provide.

Observations
The theme of godly living and good works has surfaced regularly in the epistle and with regard to women it has appeared at 2:8-10, 15; 3:11. It now comes again at 5:9, 10 and all these verses together reveal the sort of behaviour Paul is looking for as conduct worthy of those in God's household.

The reputation of the church family comes into view especially at 5:7, 8 and 5:14 and links in with similar concerns at 2:2; 3:7 and the anxiety Paul expresses about the damage being done by the false teachers. This is linked to the work of Satan at both 3:7 and 5:14f.

Exposition
The structure highlighted both for the whole section and for this sub-section is enormously helpful in guiding the way an expository treatment of this passage could work.

The church is to relate as a family (5:1, 2)
Based on the teaching of the Lord Jesus Christ that anyone who does God's will is His mother, brother and sister (see Mark 3:34, 35), we see Paul developing the notion of the church membership as a set of family relationships. This has already been hinted at earlier (see 3:4, 5) as the overseer needs to be someone who can manage and lead his own family precisely because it is a microcosm of the church family. It is of interest to note that later in this section (5:17) the church leaders are no longer termed 'overseers' but 'elders'. Given that these may be virtually identical terms (see

Acts 20:17, 28; Titus 1:5-7), the reason for Paul's change in terminology may be because he wanted to highlight the correspondence between how one treats 'older men' within the church family and 'elders' (the words in Greek are very similar and highlight the fact that in general elders would be drawn from the older men of the congregation). The main thrust is for church members to treat other believers as members of their own family. Given that the basic way in which people are to relate to their father and mother is by honouring them, it is no surprise that 'honour' is to be the main controlling characteristic of all relationships within the church family. This is developed at 5:3, 17 and 6:1, 2.

Often it is helpful to ask why Paul felt the need to give the specific instructions he gave. Could it be that some of the older men/elders were being rebuked harshly, either because of their role within the false teaching prevalent at Ephesus, or because the fall-out from the false teaching had led to the sort of behaviour, described later at 6:3-5, characterised by anger, quarrelling and friction, so that harsh language was becoming an accepted way of behaving within the church? With regard to the younger women there are several references for the need for purity (see 4:12; 5:2, 22). Perhaps the background of the false teaching and the ban on marriage (4:3) had something to do with this through denying normal sexual relationships.

The general guidelines provided by 5:1, 2 are clear and function as an introduction to the whole section 5:1–6:2. Each relationship within the church family is to mirror the ways in which people ought to treat each other as members of their own family.

The church family must care for its members in need (5:3-16)
The basic point is introduced at the outset (5:3), that
in a society with no welfare state or financial safety net
provision, widows who are in real need must be honoured
and cared for by the church family. It is interesting to note
that each time 'honour' is used it is within the context of the
need for adequate financial provision. Widows need adequate
financial and material assistance to survive (5:3). Elders who
labour at preaching and teaching need to be provided for with
some sort of financial assistance (5:17, 18) and honouring an
employer enables them to receive financial benefits from the
service of their employees (6:1, 2).

To honour widows in real need is not simply a matter
of recognising their status but has important practical
and financial consequences for the church family. In
encouraging such support, Paul is doing nothing more than
applying Old Testament provisions (e.g. Exod. 22:22) and
New Testament practices (e.g. Acts 6:1ff) to the church at
Ephesus. The question is how such care should be provided
and by whom. Paul helpfully summarises his teaching in
a conclusion at 5:16. The primary responsibility should fall
on the family of the widow (see 5:16a) and this is developed
at 5:4-8. If the widow has no family who can take care of
her, then the church family should act because she is in real
need (5:16b) and this is the point of the church's list of
widows referred to at 5:9-15.

Care from the widow's own family (5:4-8)
If the widow has any family, such as children or
grandchildren who are believers, then they should make
appropriate provision. This is a matter of putting one's
religion into practice which is pleasing to God (5:4). Failing
to do this would reflect terribly on their faith within the

wider community (5:7) and it would amount effectively to
a denial of their belief (5:8). Within 1 Timothy, faith can
be shipwrecked or abandoned through taking on board the
teachings of the false teachers (see 1:19; 4:1), but it can also
be denied through lack of love for an elderly widow within
one's family.

Once again, then, we see Paul encouraging godliness
in the form of loving provision for the elderly which is
pleasing to God and discouraging anything that would
affect the reputation of the church and the gospel within
the community.

It is therefore only in situations where there is no family
member around in the church that the church family
should be involved in providing assistance. Yet there is
one other thing that Paul adds. Within 5:5, 6 he defines
who is the widow who is really in need. These are widows
who are all alone and who rely completely on God for
assistance (5:5), in contrast to widows who are living for
their own pleasure (5:6). The latter are not in real need at
all and supporting them would be the means of the church
condoning sin which would affect the church's reputation
in the community. Paul is giving wise advice to the church
whilst encouraging proper provision for those in need. He
is not seeking indiscriminate assistance for every widow
who is on her own, since he could not countenance the idea
of a church funding immoral lifestyles. But he is forcing the
church to pay attention to the situation of widows who are
in desperate need, for whom the loving church family could
and should be the answer to their prayers (see 5:5). Here
we see Paul's blend of wisdom and compassion.

So, the first question has been raised by Paul: does this
widow have believing family members who can take care of

her, or is she really all alone and in great need? If there is no-one around and she is a godly widow crying out for help then the church family should assist. But there is another key factor which needs to be considered in 5:9-15.

Care from the widow's church family (5:9-15)

Having identified widows who have no immediate family, the church is to draw up a list so that it can administer appropriate assistance. Some commentators have argued that this list constitutes an order of ministry within the church. On this view, the widows would receive financial provision and in return they would continue their acts of service within the church family such as those identified at 5:10 and perhaps exemplified by someone such as Dorcas, known for her good deeds and assistance to the poor (see Acts 9:36, 39). This view gathers some force when considering the matter of the pledge in 5:11, 12. Could it be that in return for assistance such widows would pledge to serve Christ which would no longer be possible if they remarried? Although this view has its supporters, it is not persuasive. Those on the list need to be above sixty years old (presumably quite old within a first century context!) and these good deeds are identified as belonging to the past (see 5:9, 10).

The alternative view is that the list referred to at 5:9 and 5:11 is simply a means of identifying those widows who were without family support who were in real need. However, the list was not to be indiscriminate. Discernment was required by the church family.

1. Who should be included on the church list of widows needing support? (5:9, 10)

Three requirements are spelt out in these verses. First and foremost there is an age restriction designed to identify the elderly widow in need who would have reached the minimum age of sixty. Second, she should have been faithful in her marriage – the requirement also commended for overseers and deacons (see 3:2, 12). Third, she should have a reputation for good deeds (literally, 'good works' as at 2:10). This reputation would have developed in the way she raised her own family, would have been enhanced by her loving concern within the church family through hospitality and acts of care and would have been visible within the wider community through her concern to help people in all sorts of difficulty.

In comparing these requirements with other lists within 1 Timothy, it can be seen that the essence of these qualities is to reveal simply whether the widow has lived as a Christian believer and the only distinctive item is that she has now reached a certain age where she now needs assistance herself. The fact that 'good works' occurs twice, at the beginning and end of the list, links in with the general tone of the Pastoral Epistles. The Christian who has been saved by Christ should be zealous for good works (e.g. Titus 2:14; 3:1, 8, 14). Such a widow should now receive appropriate care through her name appearing on the list. This would represent a practical means of enabling such women who could not support themselves financially to receive the assistance they required.

2.   Who should not be included on the church list? (5:11-15)
In parallel to the three requirements for those on the list, Paul offers the reasons which separately and together should lead the church not to include such people on their

support list. First, consideration needs to be given to the age of the widow. Regardless of the fact that they might not have any family member to care for them, if they were under sixty then they should not be included (see 5:11a). As will be seen, such younger widows do not fall, generally speaking, into the category of being in real need.

Second, sexual fidelity is again important and Paul is concerned with the real possibility of such younger widows being overcome by their sexual desires (see 5:11b, 12). In attempting to reconstruct what was happening at Ephesus, it may be that younger widows in financial need had been put on the list in order to receive support but, in return, had pledged not to marry. This may have been sound common sense to avoid a situation where the church was found to be supporting a widow who had now remarried and who therefore had a husband to support her. However, it may have come about through the false teaching of some of the church leaders who were forbidding marriage (see 4:3). Not being permitted to marry within the church family, perhaps some younger widows on the list who had pledged not to marry had decided to get married anyway. It is possible that Paul is simply concerned that they have now broken their pledge (see NIV). However it could well be that through marrying they had actually abandoned their former faith (see ESV) and this may imply that this had happened through marrying a non-Christian. As a result of abandoning the faith Paul indicates that they were bringing judgement on themselves.

Such a reconstruction makes sense of the context (false teachers prohibiting marriage at church) and helps us to make some sense of verses 11, 12. If the ESV is followed at this point these younger widows had not necessarily given a pledge not to remarry. Instead they may have simply remarried in such a way as to turn from their faith in Christ, perhaps through marrying a non-Christian. Given the pro-marriage views of Paul expressed at 5:14 it is unlikely that he would have extracted from any widow a pledge not to marry. This latter reconstruction appears to be slightly more plausible though both views have their merits.

Third, as before, Paul is concerned about the reputation of the church. In contrast to the widows who should be on the list, whose lives have been characterised by good works (5:10), Paul draws to our attention the fact that some of these younger widows were idle and were known not for good works but for their many words (see 5:13). Again the context of the false teaching is important. Since marriage was now forbidden (see 4:3) the normal course of marrying and starting a family had been denied to them and in addition perhaps their speech and behaviour were beginning to mirror what they saw in some of their church leaders (see 1:4, 6; 6:3-5, 20). Living such unproductive lives certainly did not enhance the reputation of the church (see 5:14b) and neither did the fact that, as a result of the false teaching, some were even wandering away from the faith to follow Satan (see 5:15 and also 1:7; 1:19f; 4:1, 2 and 6:20, 21).

Against the backdrop of the false teaching, Paul cautions the church family against putting younger widows on the list who were damaging the reputation of the church. Instead, his positive instructions cut completely against what the false teachers were saying and at 5:14 he encourages them to marry, raise children and manage their homes. He certainly wants them to be provided for, but this need not be done by the church family. Instead, it should be through the church

family honouring the institution of marriage and enabling
the women to re-marry and start their own families. These
women were as much victims of the teaching that had swept
through Ephesus as anything else and at 5:14 we see Paul's
main concerns, mirroring his comments at 5:9, to the older
widows. Christians are to be known, whether old or young,
male or female, for their fidelity within marriage and for
their good works, which includes, for women, bearing and
raising children (and see 2:15 for this same emphasis). In
contrast to a gullible church spending money on behaviour
that promotes sin, which in turn affects the reputation of
the church in the community, the church needs to affirm
God's good gifts in creation, which includes the promotion
of marriage, and seek to encourage people to live godly lives
demonstrated in good works, which have a positive effect on
the surrounding community. Here we see all the elements
of Paul's vision for the church at Ephesus combining. First,
there is God's truth accepted and applied. Second, there is
the call for godliness to be demonstrated in good works.
Third, there is the desire for the church to have a positive
reputation within the community which will enable the
gospel to be displayed. Each of these elements feature in his
handling of this practical issue of how and when to provide
assistance for widows.

In summary, the apostle wants all older women within the
church family to be treated as mothers and so all, whether
single, widowed or married, should be honoured and
respected. Within this category he is particularly concerned
about the lack of financial provision for some widows and
the over-provision, as he sees it, of others. Believers need
to ensure that they are putting their faith into practice by

caring for widows within their family. Younger widows need to be willing to embrace a life in which they accept with thankfulness God's gift of marriage so that they are able to live lives pleasing to God and caring for others. Older widows who really do need support and who have faithfully lived for Christ should receive loving provision from the church family.

Paul reveals a mixture of compassion and discernment guided by a principled concern for the truth of God's Word (God's gift in creation and redemption), the application of God's truth to the lives of believers (godliness in action revealed in good works) and the transformation of the community through the enhanced reputation of the church and the gospel. The reputation of the church and the gospel is supremely important for Paul for its advance. This is done through preaching (see 2:7; 4:13; 5:17) but also through the godly lives of Christians. In this particular context that will mean the church family supporting and encouraging marriage, caring for the elderly within the family and making provision for those in real need, such as the elderly widows who are on their own. The church family must not take over from the widow's family but it is to be there to provide when there is no-one else. Here is love and wisdom in action, encouraging and strengthening family life and church family life in order to adorn the gospel.

Though Paul has highlighted these particular areas to Timothy because they had become issues at Ephesus, the principles that guided him have a far wider application. A concern for the truth, godly living and the reputation of the church for the sake of the gospel gives us a framework to help the church in every generation work out how to address many of the practical issues that it faces.

From text to teaching

Get the message clear

Big idea (theme)
The church family is to act with discernment and compassion to care for those within the church who are in real need.

Big questions (aim)
Preaching or teaching on this passage should answer the following questions:

1. How important is it as Christians to be involved in caring for elderly parents?

2. To what extent is godly living observed in very ordinary ways within the home, church and community?

3. How important is it for the church to act with discernment as well as compassion in situations of need?

Engage the hearer

Point of contact
Friction in a car engine leads to over-heating and eventually to breakdown. Often what is needed is oil in order to reduce the friction and enable the engine to function properly. Friction between different people and groups was clearly an issue at Ephesus (see 6:5) and so what was needed was something that would act as a lubricant in order to reduce the heat and enable the church to move forward. Paul offers the idea of 'honour' as the oil to enable the church family to live and work together far more comfortably. Loving relationships through the practical caring for the needs of

others will work like oil in the engine to provide a far more comfortable journey.

Main illustration

When visiting someone's home you might often see an array of pictures or photographs with perhaps one or two having pride of place on the mantelpiece or occupying a prominent place on a wall. The photograph is honoured by being lifted up and as a result the people on the photo are recognised as being of real importance to them. In a similar way people within a church family are honoured and respected by being lifted up and recognised. Rather than being forgotten and marginalised they are noticed, so that their needs can be identified and met. Perhaps this is a particularly important point concerning elderly people within the church family.

Application

Our relationships within the church family are meant to be modelled on family relationships. All too often relationships in the church can be far too distant and remote and so bear little resemblance to a family. Alternatively, due to the way in which our society has come to celebrate youth, energy, fashion and informality, elderly people can be forgotten, or treated with little honour, unlike other societies where the elderly are given much respect. This tendency can also be prevalent in our churches, where the emphasis can often fall on ministry amongst children, youth, students and families. As a church family, we are meant to offer a different vision of how relationships should work and giving due respect and honour to those older than us within the church is a good place to start.

We need to discern those within the church family who are genuinely in need. The needs may be financial, or may relate to practical assistance around the home, or assistance with shopping. Having identified such needs, it is then important to see whether there are family members who can assist rather than automatically assume that all needs must be met from within the church family. The church should be seeking to develop and enhance family life and responsibility rather than undercut or replace the family. In particular cases however, where there is no family, the church should consider whether there need to be social and/or financial structures put into place to provide the necessary support. Perhaps the person could be linked with another individual or family or home group. Perhaps the church could set up a Fellowship Fund which is able to assist in cases of hardship. The important point seen in the passage is that when the church family needs to help, it must be about far more than loving words but should also include practical assistance and care.

Greater social mobility means that many people now live at a distance from their parents' home. The provisions of the welfare state also mean that most people have access to various forms of provision whether from social services or the health service. Combining these things together, and adding the busy lives that people have, mean that elderly parents often receive only the most perfunctory care from their children and indeed can be entirely neglected. As Christians it is important for us to reflect and act on the command to honour our parents. This must mean a desire to seek to provide practical help when such assistance is required, whether our parent is a believer or not. For us to be busily involved in the service of the church and, at the same time, neglectful of an elderly parent should be of great concern within the community.

The reputation of the gospel is linked with the reputation of the church. For the church to have a poor reputation in a community will have a serious effect on its witness. Its reputation will be correspondingly enhanced as the church family functions as a wise and caring family, full of compassion and good works. Jesus spoke about disciples being like salt and light (Matthew 5:13-16) making a real difference through their behaviour as well as their word. Any evangelistic strategy that pays no attention at all to the godliness of the church members is almost certain to fail, whereas a church family characterised by a practical concern for one another and for those within the community will be enormously attractive.

Paul is unashamedly pro-marriage and pro-family in this passage. Of course the church needs to handle these things sensitively, recognising that within its members are people who are single, those who cannot have children and those whose experience of marriage has been dreadful. Nevertheless, marriage and the family were instituted by God as part of His good creation and it is important therefore as a church that we support and uphold these precious things. Though living in a society where there are many threats to marriage and family life, Christians are to be at the forefront of celebrating these good gifts that we have received from God.

We can make the mistake in thinking that a life pleasing to God is all about praying more and spending more time in 'spiritual' activities. There is nothing wrong in prayer (as Paul has shown at 2:1ff) but a life that pleases God is intensely practical rather than super-spiritual. It will involve caring for parents (5:4), showing hospitality and caring for the needs of those both within and outside the church family (5:10). Though apparently ordinary, these are to be the marks of genuine Christianity.

Proclaiming the message/suggestions for preaching

A preaching outline

Title: **Godly living within the church family – caring for those in need**

Text: **1 Timothy 5:1-16**

1. The church is to relate as a family 5:1, 2

2. The church family must care for its members in need 5:3-16

    a. care from the widow's own family 5:4-8

    b. care from the widow's church family 5:9-15

        • who should be included on the list for support? 5:9, 10

        • who should not be included on the list for support? 5:11-15

Other preaching possibilities:

The above exposition has sought to work through the passage in a straightforward manner. However, one could tackle the material in a different way in order to emphasise points that feature within the passage, but which are not so evident from the headings in the outline. For example, it would be possible to look at the whole passage through the lens of the reputation of the church since this is clearly an important issue in Paul's mind referred to near the end of both major paragraphs (5:7, 14).

1. How to gain a poor reputation for the gospel within the community:

    • Families failing to care for their elderly members (5:4-8)

+ Believers failing to give evidence of good works in their lives (5:11-15)

2. How to develop a good reputation for the gospel within the community:

+ Honouring and respecting the elderly through ... the family (5:3-8) ... the church family (5:9, 10).

+ Upholding marriage and family life (5:9, 10, 14)

Another possibility would be to link these verses with the following material in order to preach the whole section in one go (5:1-6:2). Clearly the disadvantage is that it means preaching on a long passage but, on the other hand, the fact that the section holds together so well with three sub-sections all beginning with the encouragement to 'honour' others does make this possible.

1. Friction within the church at Ephesus and its result.

+ Widows (5:3-16)

+ Elders (5:17-25)

+ Masters (6:1-2)

2. Honouring one another within the church family.

+ Widows (5:3-16)

+ Elders (5:17-25)

+ Masters (6:1-2)

A final possibility is to divide up the material into two sections 5:1-8 and 9-16 in order to spend more time on this passage by preaching it in two sermons:

Sermon 1: Honouring one another in the family and the church family (5:1-8)

Sermon 2: Two ways to live (5:9-16)

Leading a Bible Study

Title: **Godly living within the church family – caring for those in need**

Text: **1 Timothy 5:1-16**

1.   Introduce the issues

   ✦ Our society is breaking itself down into smaller and smaller units resulting in many more people living on their own facing isolation and loneliness. In what ways can the church be good news to those who are in great need?

2.   Study the passage

   ✦ In practical terms how does Paul want church members to relate to each other? (5:1, 2)

   ✦ From the passage, what defines whether a widow is really in need? (5:3, 5, 9, 10)

   ✦ Why do you think Paul uses such strong language at 5:4, 8 concerning failure to assist a widow?

   ✦ Is there anything surprising about Paul's list in 5:9, 10?

   ✦ Can you reconstruct what might have been happening in 5:11, 12?

   ✦ Overall, what does Paul want to see in the church at Ephesus? (5:13-16)

3. Think it through

+ How could your church become more of a genuine family?

+ Why do you think that for many of us the instructions about families caring for their elderly in 5:4, 8, 16 strike an uncomfortable note and what should we seek to do about it?

+ How can we honour the role of bringing up children more within our church family? (5:10, 14)

+ Why is Paul so concerned for the reputation of the church?

4. Live it out

+ In what ways could we care for people in real need within our own church family? What do we need to do?

+ What sort of behaviour would enhance the reputation of the church within our community?

2. Godly living within the Church family: Supporting leaders and working faithfully in the workplace (5:17–6:2)

Introduction
The whole section 5:1–6:2 develops the main thrust of 3:15 and the call for godly living – conduct worthy of those living in the household of God. Such godly living is to be worked out on the basis of viewing all relationships within the church as in a family setting (5:1, 2), in order that the church may begin to function properly as a church family.

The previous passage dealt with the problem of the lack of care for widows within the church family and now Paul proceeds to consider two other areas of tension within the fellowship relating to elders in the church and masters in the workplace. Paul's aim is to enable each of these relationships to be considered from the angle of family relationships and his concern is that members should show honour and respect to each other. These are important roles that need to be performed both in church and in the workplace but they are to be viewed within the basic guidelines concerning how a Christian family is to function in a manner pleasing to God.

Listening to the text

Context, structure and observations

Context

This section is highly structured. From the opening few verses which reveal how the church is to operate as a family (5:1, 2) Paul considers three particular relationships in which honour or respect is to be shown (5:3, 17; 6:1). The context must take into account what had been happening within the church with the rise of the false teachers. One can easily see that with the controversies and arguments that flowed from their teaching (1:4; 6:4, 5), there could have been severe tensions between the leadership and the whole church family. This may lead to the unwillingness of some church members to pay their ministers ('Why should we pay people who are departing from the truth and stirring up all these difficulties?'). Had it led to a culture where church leaders were being fired quickly because of their beliefs or behaviour? Had this then led to the over-hasty appointment of new church leaders and had this in the end exacerbated the problems even more? It is not easy to be certain, but the presence of the false teachers and the difficult struggle going on within the leadership at Ephesus, as considered at 1:18-20, do help us to see why some of these issues needed to be tackled.

Structure
Both parts of this passage reveal a structure to Paul's thoughts, which is also linked to the opening verses of the whole section in 5:1, 2.

1. Elders are to be treated like fathers (5:17-25)

   + they are to be honoured (5:17, 18)

   + don't remove them too quickly (5:19-21)

   + don't appoint them too hastily (5:22-25)

2. Masters are to be treated like brothers (6:1, 2)

   + they are to be honoured (6:1, 2)

   + ... so that the reputation of the gospel is advanced (6:1) (unbelieving masters?)

   + ... so that the brother in Christ benefits (6:2) (believing masters)

Observations
There are several links with other parts of the epistle which reveal that this is a key passage in Paul's letter. Primarily, we see the focus on leadership issues which Paul has referred to at 1:18-20; 2:11-15; 3:1-13 and 4:6-16. The problems caused by false teaching arising from some within the church leadership has meant that such leadership issues must be addressed. The change of terminology from overseer in 3:1ff to elder or presbyter at 5:17 can be explained from

a number of angles. First, it is likely that the two terms were identical on the basis of Acts 20:17, 28 and Titus 1:5-7, where in both cases only one group of leaders is being referred to, though at least two different titles are used. Second, it may be that Paul wants to provide a clear link between the way other men should be honoured within the church family (5:1) and how the elders are to be honoured (5:17). The words for 'older men' and 'elder' are extremely similar deriving from the same root and there would have been a large overlap between the two groups, since most, if not all, the elders would be likely to be drawn from the older men within the church family.

Other connecting links include the following:

1. the reputation of the church and how its members operate is of tremendous importance to Paul in this section (5:7, 14, 20; 6:1).

2. the purity of church members, and perhaps especially the male leaders, is of concern to Paul in terms of how they were relating to the younger Christian women (4:12; 5:2, 22).

3. Paul reacts to counter the ascetic tendency in the church revealed at 4:3 which may be why he inserts into his direct teaching to Timothy advice about drinking wine (5:23).

The section begins and ends by referring to relationships within the church family. Younger men are to be treated as brothers (5:1) and believing masters are also to be treated as brothers who are dear to you (6:2). This church family brotherly relationship must neither be ignored (5:1), nor abused (6:2). This ties the whole section together.

Exposition

Basing this exposition on the structure of the passage, there are two main parts though considerably more material to cover in the first part relating to elders.

Honouring leaders in the church (5:17-25)

Paying leaders too little (5:17, 18)

It is helpful to interrogate the text by asking a series of questions which enable the details of the passage to be uncovered.

1. How are leaders described?

They are described as elders in contrast to the overseer described earlier in the epistle (see 3:1-7). As mentioned above, the word for elder is almost identical to 'older men' (see 5:1).

2. What do they do?

Two distinct roles are described by Paul and one of the issues concerns whether this represents two types of elder or two aspects of the same ministry. First, they are involved in directing (NIV) or ruling (ESV) the church family. The root word has already appeared at 3:4, 5, 12 and 5:14 and is often translated as 'manage'. It seems to be a word linked to those in charge of Christian congregations from the earliest days (see 1 Thess. 5:12). It picks up the idea of authority required in any leadership position, whether in the home or the church. The elders are the people who lead, make decisions, exercise authority and seek to run the church. Second, there are elders who work or labour in preaching and teaching. Again, the idea of labour and hard work is linked with the leadership role at 1 Thess. 5:12, but here it is specified as being linked to preaching and teaching. This role is an important part of ministry for Paul (see 2:7), Timothy (see 4:13) and the overseer (see 3:2).

It is possible that there are 'ruling' elders and 'preaching' elders, on the basis that 5:17 may refer to the latter category as being a subset of the former. Though this may be the case, it is possible that the phrase 'especially those who work in preaching and teaching' does not denote different people but a different aspect of the same role. The word translated 'especially' has also appeared at 4:10 and 5:8 and in both cases it may simply be a means of emphasising a particular point (e.g. at 4:10 the living God is the Saviour of those who trust Him; at 5:8 it is a denial of faith for church members not to provide for their immediate relatives). If that is the case here, the verse may be highlighting that the main way that the elders direct the church is through the means of working hard at preaching and teaching. Seen in this light there are no longer two types of elder. Rather, we see the elder, like the overseer, as the person who, along with other overseers or elders, leads the church through preaching God's Word. Of course that does not mean that we don't need people involved within the overall leadership who have gifts of administration or steering the church in the right direction etc. (see 1 Cor. 12:28; Rom. 12:8), but it does mean that we should clarify the point that leadership comes through (literally) 'the word and teaching' (see 5:17). This understanding would also serve to bring 5:17 into line with the rest of the New Testament material about elders since at no other point is there reference to two types of elder.

3. What should they receive?

These elders are to receive double honour. It is more than simply being respected for their hard work. At other points 'honour' appears to have a financial connotation as at 5:3 for the widow in need and 6:1, 2 for the master to receive a benefit from the slave's work. Here the reference is to 'double' honour which may reflect both respect together with a financial element i.e. honour plus an honorarium. Certainly 5:18 picks up the note of providing some material reward to these elders. It is interesting to note in passing that Paul quotes both from the Old Testament (Deut. 25:4) and Jesus' words from the gospel (Luke 10:7) indicating that the gospels had already become part of the scriptures. The images used in the verses selected by Paul are not particularly flattering to the preacher: he is likened to a lumbering ox going round and round in circles as it treads out the grain and he is also described as a labourer going about his work. Both images speak of the hard work and labour involved in a regular, weekly ministry of preaching as well as indicating that some sort of payment is appropriate to those who have given their best efforts to this ministry.

Perhaps the idea of 'double honour' is to highlight the respect that the office of elder should command in a similar way to Paul's earlier observation that the role of the overseer is a noble task or good work (see 3:1). Perhaps it was necessary to underline these things because of the dishonour brought on the roles due to the activity and behaviour of the false teachers (see 1:3-7; 6:3-5). Though some had brought the teaching ministry of the church into disrepute, those who have been raised up as elders and who were doing the task well should be particularly respected. And Paul's point is that this respect should be reflected in some form of payment, in order to enable the leader to continue to devote all his energies to this role (see 4:13; 5:17).

Firing leaders too quickly 5:19-21

1. What was happening at Ephesus?
Paul seems to include this material at this point because of accusations being levelled at some of the leaders in the

church, which had led to their instant dismissal. It is not easy to understand exactly what was happening. Were some of the false teachers and their supporters stirring up trouble for the other leaders? Or were leaders being held in such low regard due to the fall-out from the false teaching that leaders were being summarily dismissed if there were even the slightest hint of controversy? Whatever the background, Paul needs to address the problem of accusations against elders leading to instant dismissal.

1. How should the church act in disciplinary cases involving church leaders?

There may well be a chiastic structure in this passage which it is helpful to be aware of in highlighting the main issues.

> A   No unwarranted accusations (5:19a)
>
> > B   Witnesses needed (5:19b) …
> > to corroborate accusation
> >
> > > C   Public rebuke (5:20)
> >
> > B   Witnesses needed (5:21a) …
> > to prevent favouritism
>
> A   No favouritism (5:21b)

There are two problems which Paul addresses. To prevent unwarranted and unsubstantiated accusations against church leaders he ensures that the facts of the complaint are corroborated by at least two or three witnesses. Given the malicious talk that was prevalent (see 6:4), it is easy to see how slanderous accusations might be made which had no basis in fact. By requesting witnesses, Paul is seeking to ensure justice, whilst also preserving the reputation of the church in the eyes of the world.

The other problem he highlights is favouritism. So, it might be possible that even though a serious accusation is made and substantiated by witnesses, it is simply brushed under the carpet due to favouritism. Perhaps some of the elders were likely to stick together in order to ensure that a fellow elder was not disciplined. Again, Paul appeals to witnesses to remind Timothy that his decisions are witnessed by God, Christ Jesus and the elect angels to ensure that he realises that there is to be no partiality in his decision making. Again, such a provision is designed to preserve the church's reputation and to protect any sort of cover up which could easily give rise to a scandal.

In the centre of the chiasm is the call for the erring elder to be rebuked publicly. On the basis that the witnesses have corroborated the accusation, and on the basis that the presence of the other witnesses in 5:21 have ensured that there is no favouritism, the elder should be disciplined. The fact that this is to be done publicly again ensures that there is no cover up and is designed to preserve the reputation of the church within the community. Presumably the sin referred to is fairly serious and deserving of a public censure rather than a private admonition. In passing it can be seen that the process bears a striking resemblance to the disciplinary code contained in Matthew 18:15-18.

Once again we can see familiar themes emerging. Paul is passionately committed to the godliness of church members and particularly church leaders in order that the reputation of the church and the gospel is enhanced rather than diminished. Serious sin must therefore be exposed and dealt with to indicate to the wider community the difference that the gospel should make to the lifestyle and behaviour of believers.

One other way of looking at the verses would be to divide up the passage in a slightly different way, though the main lessons will remain the same:

A.   Accusations of sin need witnesses 5:19

B.   Sin should be rebuked publicly 5:20

C.   Sin should not be covered up 5:21

The advantage of considering the passage in this way is that it puts the emphasis at the end which explains the solemn charge given to Timothy at the beginning of 5:21. Further, in the contemporary church this is one of the main scandals, where sins have been covered up due to partiality or favouritism.

Hiring leaders too hastily 5:22-25

1. What was happening at Ephesus?
We know from the evidence of 1:19, 20 that some of the false teachers had already been dismissed. Further, the preceding verses have highlighted that some of the elders may have required either discipline or dismissal from their posts (5:19-21). In such a situation it would be a straightforward reaction to appoint new leaders immediately in order to ensure continuation of the important ministry of the elders. However, both here at 5:22 and previously at 3:6 Paul flags up the danger of doing this too quickly. People need time to mature (see 3:6) and the process of appointment needs time for the appropriate examination and weighing up of the character of candidates for this office (see 5:22ff).

2. How should the church act in appointing new church leaders?

Paul passes on two pieces of advice to Timothy about the process of appointments.

+ Take care 5:22, 23

If you appoint somebody as a church leader who is not appropriate for the task and who causes damage to the church due to their teaching or behaviour, which then causes others to abandon the faith or make shipwreck of their faith (1:19; 4:1), then you bear responsibility for what happens. You stand alongside the other elders who laid hands on the new leader at their commissioning (see 1:18 and 4:14 for Timothy's experience of commissioning) in sharing responsibility and all of you must be held accountable for this new leader's sinful ways. Paul encourages Timothy therefore to take great care in appointing leaders so that he does not find himself embroiled in their sins. By contrast, he has to keep himself pure, unstained from the corruption of others.

At this point, Paul inserts a parenthetical statement which makes sense when understood within its context. Having encouraged Timothy to keep himself pure, Paul doesn't want Timothy to get the wrong end of the stick and to think that this is all about following certain rules, as perhaps envisaged by the false teachers themselves at 4:3. Genuine purity is not about keeping man-made laws which have the effect of denying God's goodness in creation. Rather, he is to use God's gifts with thanksgiving (see 4:4) which includes the imbibing of a little wine to assist Timothy in his health.

This verse signals Timothy's weak physical constitution, which may of course have been the result of bearing all the pressures of ministerial responsibility at Ephesus. Perhaps the weighty responsibility of appointing leaders was a particular concern and this had adversely affected his health. Certainly the demands of leadership, including the hard work described in 5:17 and implied at 5:18, are considerable and it would be no surprise if these things had contributed to his physical weakness.

The main point is that Timothy needs to take great care in the appointment of church leaders so that he is not in any way responsible for false teaching or ungodly behaviour entering the church.

+ Take time 5:24, 25

The other instruction, already implied in the command not to be hasty (see 5:22), is to take time in weighing up the character and behaviour of a potential candidate for church leadership. Though a tree can look spectacular in spring covered in blossom, it is no guarantee that it will produce good fruit later in the year. Fruit takes time to grow and so it not safe simply to judge by appearances. This works in two ways.

First, with regard to sin, sometimes its presence in a church leader is obvious, perhaps because it is exposed by the list at 3:2ff (e.g. drunkenness or a volatile temper). But sometimes sin only becomes apparent afterwards, perhaps like purchasing a second-hand car which apparently measured up to all the right standards, but a few months later starts to break down on a regular basis. In the same way only time can reveal whether the candidate for leadership leaves behind a trail of good works or of sinful actions.

It is the same concerning good works, which has been a recurring theme within the letter (see 2:10, 5:10). They may be obvious and apparent immediately. On the other hand, if you take time, you will also be able to observe other good deeds emerging as they come to the surface. The point is clear. As Timothy takes time in the discernment process, so other information will surely come to light which is likely to provide significant help in deciding whether someone should be appointed to a position of church leadership.

Overall then, Paul is encouraging caution concerning the commissioning of leaders. As in the parable of the Sower and the soils (Mark 4:1ff), it is not immediately clear how the seed will develop, so Timothy must take care and take time in order to discern who should be the appropriate new church leaders required in Ephesus.

In summary, church leaders are to be honoured for their work for the gospel through adequate provision and their position should be respected in such a way that elders are not dismissed lightly nor appointed hastily. It is an important office within the church that demands great care and attention in terms of who is appointed and whether they should be dismissed.

Honouring employers in the workplace (6:1, 2)
It needs to be recognised that there is no direct equivalent between first century slavery and modern employment practices and therefore great care needs to be taken in speaking of employers rather than masters. Equal care needs to be taken if the master/slave terminology is retained, recognising that first century slavery was also very different from nineteenth century forms of slavery. The slave trade which forcibly transferred multitudes of Africans to the other side of the Atlantic was a dreadful evil and is very different from the relationships that Paul envisages in this letter. However, the important thing to recognise is that there are important principles highlighted in the text which can and should be applied to our context rather than left behind due to differences in employment practices.

Showing respect to the boss (6:1, 2)

Twice in this passage Paul uses the word for honour or respect which ties this passage to the others within this section (see 5:3, 17; 6:1, 2). Whether the boss is a Christian (6:2), or not (6:1), respect is to be shown. As before, respect or honour has financial connotations – the widow, the elder and now the boss at work are all to benefit from the believer within the church family. In this case the benefit comes from the service provided to the employer to enable their business to prosper.

Showing respect ... so that the reputation of the gospel is not damaged (6:1).

Whether the boss in 6:1 is a Christian or not is unclear, though the fact that 6:2 specifically refers to a believing master lends weight to the idea that 6:1 refers to the situation where the boss is not a believer. The important point is that the reason given for showing respect is that 'God's name and our teaching may not be slandered'. Once again, this chimes in with a theme that Paul has regularly highlighted at 2:2; 3:7; 5:7, 14 concerning the reputation of the church within the community. Specifically here it is God's own reputation and 'the teaching' which is in view which adds force to Paul's statement. Perhaps the temptation for the Christian slave at that time was to question why they should have to work so hard under the yoke of slavery and bring benefit to their master, given that he may be hostile to the faith. The response is that to show respect by working hard will commend God's name and the gospel and perhaps be the means of advancing both. Whereas to show little respect by working half-heartedly would have the effect of significantly hindering the work of the gospel. As so often is the case, Paul sees godliness not just as a response to the gospel (see 1:5) but as a means of promoting the gospel.

Showing respect ... so that the brother in Christ benefits (6:2)
With a Christian master the temptation might come
in a different form. Since he is a brother (see 5:1), it is
reasonable to think that, as Christians within the church
family, you have the same status. Since that is true, your
brother should be forgiving and kind and will therefore
tolerate slightly less commitment in the workplace,
especially if the reason for your shorter hours is your
involvement in church meetings. Surely he is bound to be
understanding. However, Paul immediately tackles such
thinking by encouraging Christian employers to work even
harder for their employer if he or she is a Christian. As
a brother in Christ he should be dear to you and further,
you should want to see him benefit and prosper. In other
words, the picture of Christians reacting to each other on
the basis of family relationships (see 5:1, 2) should not be
an excuse for over-familiarity and less respect, but should
be an encouragement to greater love and concern.

How you act in the workplace first affects the reputation
of the gospel within the community and second is meant
to demonstrate the reality of a loving church family. In
including this short section, Paul is in fact summarising
his two main points in the entire section as they relate to
the treatment of widows and elders as well. The watching
world should be able to observe something which attracts
them to the gospel and this is done particularly when
believers honour one another by showing love and making
provision for each other. No wonder Paul concludes this
section by getting Timothy to teach and to urge these
things on the church family. Slackness and lack of love in
your relationships within the church family will adversely
affect the progress of the gospel; whereas if believers live

godly lives, honouring each other, then the truth of the gospel is put on display for all to see. Seen in this way, the whole section 5:1–6:2 flows from Paul's key aim revealed particularly at 3:15. Knowing how to conduct oneself as a Christian within God's family or household will enable the truth to be lifted up.

From text to teaching

Get the message clear

Big idea (theme)
Church leaders and employers need to be honoured and respected for the sake of the reputation of the gospel.

Big questions (aim)
Preaching or teaching on this passage should answer the following questions:

1. In what ways should churches seek to honour their leaders?

2. What should be the main considerations in selecting and appointing church leaders?

3. In what way is the reputation of the gospel linked to the behaviour of believers?

Engage the hearer

Point of contact
Football managers in the Premiership are often hired and fired at an alarmingly fast rate. Some managers are simply not given a chance after a poor result and mistakes are then made because of the need to appoint a successor quickly. Though church leadership is very different (as are the salaries!), it highlights the danger of a hiring and

firing mentality and the need for carefully thought-through appointments to be made, which will stand the test of time.

Main illustration

If you were needing to purchase a second-hand car you would want far more than a cursory inspection and a brief recommendation. If that is all you have, then you wouldn't be surprised if you encountered major problems sometime later. Indeed, it would be far better not to make the purchase but to spend time, effort and money, on a detailed examination in order to see if the car will keep going for the coming years. How much more is it important for potential church leaders to be examined carefully over a period of time, rather than making a snap judgement?

Application

It needs to be recognised that preaching and teaching involves hard work. It should involve hard work for the preacher to seek to live a godly life (see 4:9) and it will certainly involve prolonged labour in preparing sermons that faithfully open up the scriptures and inspire hearers. We should not be surprised at meeting pastors who are struggling under this burden because it is a relentless task. Though it is an enormous privilege to serve Christ in this way, the labour involved needs to be recognised and appropriately rewarded.

Great discernment is required in the whole area of church discipline and especially in the area of handling situations involving church leaders. For many years a number of prominent denominations have singularly failed to discipline, and issues appear to have been swept under the carpet. Though it is obviously important to be wise and sensitive in establishing whether discipline is called for, nevertheless if it is required, the church needs to act, or face great harm to its reputation.

Discernment is also required in the selection of candidates for church leadership. One of the dangers in some denominations is that decisions are made which may not take sufficient notice of areas relating to Christian character and behaviour. Time is needed in this process and candidates should not be too frustrated if the process of discernment takes longer than they had anticipated. Further, such decisions need to be taken by those who know the candidate well. Courage is needed sometimes to reject candidates; it is much better for this to happen than that false teaching, or abhorrent behaviour, spreads through the church as a result of the appointment.

Christians in the workplace are on the front line concerning whether the reputation of the gospel suffers or is enhanced. They need encouragement to see that they play a critical role in the advance of the gospel through their willingness to work hard whilst displaying a godly character.

Christians need to view being part of the church family as an enormous privilege. It should also be the means of encouraging greater love and respect between one another precisely because we are part of the same family headed by Christ.

Proclaiming the message/suggestions for preaching

A preaching outline

Title: **Godly living within the church family – supporting leaders and working faithfully in the workplace**

Text: **1 Timothy 5:17–6:2**

1.   Honouring leaders in the church (5:17-25)

   ✦   through providing appropriate payments (17, 18) (the danger of paying leaders too little)

   ✦   through giving wise judgements (19-21) (the danger of firing leaders too quickly)

+ through making discerning appointments (22-25) (the danger of hiring leaders too quickly)

2. Honouring employers in the workplace (6:1, 2)

+ Showing respect to the boss 6:1, 2

+ ... so that the reputation of the church is not damaged 6:1

+ ... so that the brother in Christ benefits 6:2

Other preaching possibilities:
One simple expedient would be to divide this material into two sermons. The advantage would be that it would enable much more time to be spent on dealing with issues relating to being a Christian in the workplace, especially as this is a subject which may not be preached on sufficiently otherwise. The disadvantage is that this sort of decision does lengthen the whole series. A further refinement could be to preach a short series of three sermons on this section (5:1-16; 5:17-25; 6:1, 2) under the heading of honouring one another within the church family.

Another possibility previously highlighted would be to gather the material together from within 1 Timothy which specifically relates to church leaders (3:1-13; 4:6-16 and 5:17-25) in order to show what sort of leadership Paul is looking for, in contrast to the false teachers.

Leading a Bible Study
Title: **Godly living within the church family – supporting leaders and working faithfully in the workplace**
Text: **1 Timothy 5:17–6:2**

1. Introduce the issues:

+ How important, for any organisation, is a good reputation?

+ What are the things which can affect its reputation either for good or ill?

2. Study the passage

    + What do you think is meant by 'double honour' in 5:17, 18?

    + What are the dangers Paul highlights in relation to disciplining church leaders? (5:19-21)

    + What are the dangers Paul highlights in relation to appointing church leaders? (5:22-25)

    + How does verse 23 relate to verse 22 in the light of the false teaching at 4:3?

    + Why might it be tempting not to work hard for a non-Christian boss (6:1)? ... or for a Christian boss (6:2)?

    + What would be the effect of not working hard in both these situations? (6:1, 2)

3. Think it through

    + In what ways do you honour or support your church leaders?

    + In the light of 5:19-21, what principles should your church use if a leader needed disciplining?

    + In the light of 5:22-25, what principles should your church use in the appointment of leaders at all levels within the fellowship?

    + What principles are transferable from the master/ slave relationship to modern employment practices?

4. Live it out

  + How can we enable the reputation of the gospel to be enhanced within our community?

  + How can we encourage each other to be faithful in the workplace as Christians?

Part 6

RESPONDING TO FALSE TEACHING

1 Timothy 6:3-21

1. The danger of turning away from the Word of Christ (6:3-10)

Introduction

As we come to Paul's final section of the epistle (6:3-21) we see him returning to his opening theme. Just as he started his opening section with a description of the false teachers (1:3ff) so he does the same at 6:3ff using the same terminology. In the intervening material Paul has sought to refocus the church in Ephesus towards the priorities of the advance of the gospel and the necessity of godliness amongst both church members and church leaders (2:1-3:13). At the centre of the letter he has sought to clarify Timothy's role in enabling these priorities to be set through his own personal example and public ministry (3:14–4:16). Following this, he has once again returned to consider some of the issues that need addressing in the Ephesian church so that it could operate as a church family, honouring one another (5:1–6:2). Now Paul returns to his opening theme which had caused him to write in the first place, which concerns how to address the problem of the false teachers.

Although he is addressing the same theme and there is a shared vocabulary that unites the opening and closing section of the letter, there is one important difference, highlighted in the table:

	Emphasis of false teaching	Response
Ch. 1	It's all about what you do – the law	Christ's first coming – look what He has done
Ch. 6	It's all about what you have – money	Christ's second coming – look what He will give

In the first part of the final section (6:3-10), Paul opens up the issues before giving his main response in the second part (6:11-21).

Listening to the text

Context, structure and observations

Context

The previous section (5:1–6:2) concluded with the words 'teach and urge these things'. It is likely that, as at 4:6, this has a backwards reference and represents a call for Timothy to apply the teaching about relationships within the church, which has characterised that portion of the letter. If so, Paul now draws a contrast between such orthodox teaching relating to godly behaviour and the false teaching which had occurred at Ephesus with its resulting ungodly behaviour (6:3-5).

Also it can be seen that, just as the first section began with a description of the false teaching (1:3-7) followed later by a call for Timothy to confront these teachers (1:18-20), so the final section has the same pattern. The issue is addressed at the start (6:3-5), and at the end Timothy is once again given a very personal charge to confront this false teaching (6:20, 21).

Structure

Commentators have often been frustrated in noting that Paul includes two sections concerning money (6:6-10 and 6:17-19) when he could have dealt with the matter in one go. However, once one recognises that Paul has very deliberately included two passages which relate to money it goes a long way to helping us to identify the structure of the whole section.

A.	The behaviour of the false teachers (6:3-5)	
	B	Handling money (6:6-10)
A	The behaviour of the true teacher (6:11-16)	
	B	Handling money (6:17-19)
A	The true teacher v. the false teachers (6:20, 21)	

It can be seen that the issue of handling money occurs twice. On both occasions it appears as a worked example and ties in with the behaviour either of the false teachers or the genuine believer. At 6:6-10 the dominant note is to warn the false teachers concerning where their handling of money will lead them. At 6:17-19 the corresponding dominant note is to encourage genuine believers how to handle their money – a very different destination indeed!

Observations

The parallels between 1:3-7 and 6:3-5 are numerous. Both refer to false teaching (1:3; 6:3), controversies (1:4; 6:4), meaningless talk/quarrels about words (1:6; 6:4) and failing to understand (1:7; 6:4). These links clearly serve to bind the opening and closing sections together.

One other prominent theme is the idea of wandering from the faith. It revealed the result of the false teaching both at the beginning and end of the first section (1:6; 1:19). Once again, in the closing section, it reveals the result of following the path of the false teaching and appears at both the start of Paul's argument and at the end (6:10; 6:21). Being deceived (by Satan) and wandering away from the faith into disobedience was also featured in the other three sections (2:14; 4:1; 5:15) and again serves to remind us that this is one of the key things which Paul is encouraging Timothy to address.

Exposition

The structure already highlighted proves to be very helpful in guiding the way an expository treatment of this material could be developed.

Rejecting the words of Christ (6:3-5)

At the beginning of the epistle Paul has shown what happens when false teaching gains ground within the church (1:3-7). It results in ungodly behaviour and people departing from the faith. In this parallel passage Paul probes deeper and spells out in more detail what happens when false teaching becomes embedded within the church. In doing this, Paul is filling out for us even further the various glimpses we have already been given of the false teachers (1:3-7; 4:1-3; 6:3-5), which helps to identify their beliefs, behaviour and motives. He is also helping Timothy to see how these false teachers have arrived at the position where they are now seeking financial gain from their ministry. So, once again, he provides an anatomy of the false teaching, dissecting things in order to reveal what is happening at the centre. And once again, as at 1:3-7, Paul employs a chiastic structure which enables us to see the main points.

A. False teaching – turning from the words of Christ 6:3

    B. The reality – such a person understands nothing 6:4a

        C. The result – a description of ungodly behaviour 6:4b,5a

    B. The reality – such a person has been robbed of the truth 6:5b

A. False teaching – embracing religion for financial gain 6:5c

The content of the false teaching (6:3, 5c)
Paul identifies their false teaching both in terms of what it rejected (6:3) and what it affirmed (6:5c). Both parts include a reference to 'godliness' though this is slightly obscured in the NIV which refers to 'godly teaching' at 6:3. So, those teaching different or false doctrines have departed from the sound or healthy words of our Lord Jesus Christ. These words of Christ are identified as 'the teaching that accords with godliness' (ESV). The false teachers are involved in teaching which has moved away from the words of Christ and genuine godly behaviour; this has been particularly characterised by their wrong thinking which has led them to the conclusion that godliness would lead to financial gain.

Unpacking the various elements, Paul contrasts the false teaching with sound or healthy teaching, which he has previously done at 1:10. In that verse, sound doctrine was linked to the glorious gospel, whereas in these verses it is associated with the words of our Lord Jesus Christ, which clearly equate to the gospel itself. These gospel words are then linked with godly teaching which embraces both the teaching of the gospel and the behaviour that results. So, in rejecting the gospel and godliness, the false teachers have betrayed the very heart of the Christian faith which is why Paul is so keen that these things are right at the top of Timothy's priorities, both for the church (see 3:15) and for himself (4:6-16).

It is no surprise then that such false teaching would lead to a different vision of godliness, which no longer accords with behaviour that honours God and one another, but which leads to personal material gain. Whereas the first characteristic identified by Paul in the false teaching was legalism (1:7 – it's all about what we do!), now he adds in materialism (6:5c – it's all about what we can get!). This would particularly apply to the teachers themselves, recognising that perhaps the situation had been exacerbated by the failure of the church to give 'double honour' to some of its leaders (see 5:17, 18) with the result that the need for material provision had become a dominant note. Either way, there is a contrast drawn between genuine leaders, who should not be lovers of money (3:4) and not pursue dishonest gain (3:8) and those referred to at 6:5c.

Though this material applies to the false teachers, their example would be observed and therefore the notion that godliness would lead to financial gain would no doubt soon spread across the church family. In contrast to the generosity within the church family that Paul has been encouraging, where honouring one another has included a financial element, we now see leaders and others within the church grasping for more. Perhaps it is also instructive to note that when Paul had addressed the church leaders of Ephesus at Miletus in Acts 20, he quoted some direct words of the Lord Jesus, 'it is more blessed to give than to receive' (Acts 20:35). These words complete a short section where Paul reveals his own practice as an example to those leaders concerning how they should consider material possessions. It is no surprise that in our passage rejecting the words of Jesus leads to the opposite conclusion, 'it is more blessed to receive than to give'!

The reality of the situation (6:4a, 5b)

In rejecting the words of Christ and embracing this view that godliness would lead to financial gain, the false teachers revealed their conceit and pride. It is staggering that people can think that they know better than Christ, yet so often this can be the case. However, rather than improving on the truth we find that the reality of the situation is that as at 1:7 these false teachers understand nothing (6:4a). Subtracting from the word of Jesus will empty out all meaning and provide people with nothing. So though in their pride they thought they knew it all, nothing could be further from the truth and this is always the way when church leaders turn away from the Scriptures. The effect on others within the church family is recorded at 6:5b – they will find that they have been robbed of the truth. Who has robbed them? It is those teaching different doctrines who have done so. It is like a situation where someone is mugged in the street and has all their articles of value taken from them leaving them with nothing. So here, these church leaders had 'mugged' the church family, taking from their possession the words of Jesus as well as material riches. No greater theft can be contemplated. In reality, these false teachers were conceited, understood nothing, depraved in their own mind (how else could you explain the process through which the words of Jesus were rejected?) and as a result had robbed the church of the truth.

The results of their teaching (6:4b, 5a)

Not only had the church been deprived of the truth, but the fallout could be observed in the behaviour of the leaders, no doubt spreading out into the church family itself. Rather like a corrupted computer programme which spreads a virus, so the corrupted minds of the church leadership had led to the spread of a virus of ungodly behaviour. The list includes controversies and quarrels which were noted before (1:4). In passing, it is worth noting that when the words of Jesus are rejected (6:3) it leads to quarrels about words. If we don't agree with Jesus' words we will soon find ourselves disagreeing about each other's words. This then leads to envy, strife, malicious talk, evil suspicions and constant friction. Paul has already warned the church about some of these characteristics (see 2:8 for anger and disputes; and 3:11 and 5:13 for malicious talk etc.) and he has particularly stressed the need for those involved in church leadership to be chosen partly on the basis of their self control in speech (see 3:2, 3; 4:12).

Perhaps the most evocative image that Paul utilises here is the idea of constant friction. We can imagine a lawnmower engine which has no oil to lubricate the various moving parts and has not been serviced for a while. When switched on the engine is noisy and soon begins to overheat due to the friction generated. As the overheating increases the likelihood is that a breakdown is just around the corner. Similarly, in a church where the words of Christ have been rejected and people have been robbed of the truth, the result will be friction between the leaders and indeed within the whole church family, which will lead to lots of noise, overheating and eventual breakdown. It is a salutary warning of the results of false teaching.

So Paul has catalogued for Timothy various aspects of the false teaching in order to warn him of the damage being caused to the church. In contrast to the characteristics of the godly overseer or deacon (3:1-13), or of Timothy himself (4:6-16), we have a portrait of apostasy. In each case Paul intertwines belief and behaviour, life and doctrine. Jumping on the wrong train out of the station will probably take you a long way from your intended destination. Similarly these false teachers had jumped on to the wrong teachings and as a result they were now reaching a destination far removed from the godly living that should flow from the gospel.

Accepting the love of money (6:6-10)

Having spelt out the dangers of the materialistic mindset of the false teachers, Paul now seeks to develop this theme. In this next passage Paul points out the right path (6:6-8), but his main point is to reveal the path which the false teachers and their followers were setting out on and its destination (6:9, 10). The structure of these verses corresponds to this division where contentment (6:6, 8) is contrasted with the desires, love and cravings for more (6:9, 10).

The path of contentment (6:6-8)

The references to contentment appear at the beginning and end of this short passage, to show where the focus of Paul's thinking lies. Having made reference to the fact that the false teachers were out for financial gain (6:5), Paul wants to show that there is tremendous gain in a godly life, but it will not necessarily include any financial rewards. Whether such material gains are received is irrelevant as far as the apostle is concerned, because one of the most important factors in living a godly life is to have contentment concerning possessions and riches. There is a striking similarity here to Philippians 4:10-13 where he also deals with this theme of contentment. So, it is godliness with a contented attitude to issues relating to wealth and poverty that will lead to great gain (6:6).

How is such an attitude possible? It is through gaining an eternal perspective (6:7). Having brought nothing into the world we can take nothing out of it. This immediately relativises any financial benefits in this life because it means (subject to 6:19 discussed later) that they have no bearing on true riches for the Christian. Any 'gain' that comes from godliness is ultimately linked to eternity and what we will receive as believers rather than on the amount we possess now.

Given this eternal perspective, we are reminded that the simple material benefits of food and clothing are all that we really need (6:8). Of course the Lord may choose to give us much more, but having an eternal perspective on this issue helps us to thank God for the basics in preparation for all the true riches of glory. Already then we are beginning to see where Paul is leading in this final section. The false teachers had become focussed on blessings in the present world, whereas for Paul these riches will only be found in eternity when Christ returns (6:11-16) and therefore the right way to handle money is to find a way of using it in order to lay up treasures for the coming age (6:17-19).

The path of craving for more (6:9, 10)
These verses trace the way and destination of the opposite pathway to contentment. Whereas contentment will lead to great gain, the lust for more will lead into danger and

ultimate disaster. 'Contentment' contrasts with desiring to be rich, loving money and craving for gain. Each of these phrases speaks of an enormous hunger for more. The 'great gain' of verse 6 is contrasted with people plunging to ruin and destruction and piercing themselves with many griefs. Each of these phrases speaks of hell in contrast to heaven and results in great loss both now and in eternity.

So, let us examine both verses separately to see how each trace out the same pathway. First, Paul refers to those who desire to be rich. They want more than they possess and so, rather than being content, they hunger for greater riches and wealth. The result in this life is that such an attitude will lead people into temptation which will cause them to be ensnared by many other desires. Rather than being satisfied with some financial or material reward, such people are ensnared, so that they constantly want more. Their appetite is never ultimately satisfied. Like bait on a fish hook, the riches looked so inviting, but after feasting on the bait you find that you have now been hooked and cannot get away. Satisfying their desires only leads to greater desires and must breed deep discontentment and unhappiness in this life. Yet, worse is to come because the end result is that this course of life will plunge people into ruin and destruction. Like someone running headlong down a steep field only to find themselves at the top of a cliff with the pounding surf below, so the pursuit of wealth eventually leads to the cliff top at the foot of which lies the depths of hell. It is a sobering picture and contrasts great gain with total loss (6:9).

This theme is repeated for emphasis in 6:10 using slightly different pictures. In contrast to contentment Paul speaks of those with a 'love of money' who are 'eager for money'.

It is a parody of the true path of godliness mentioned at the beginning of the letter, where we were told that the goal of God's work is love (1:5). But rather than a love for others these individuals are consumed by a love for money. Where will this lead? Again we see the consequences both now and in eternity. The love of money is pictured as a root from which all sorts of evil grow. Some of these things have already been described in 6:4, 5 but Paul's main concern is that this sort of desire will lead to people wandering from the faith. Perhaps being blinded by the lure of riches they wander off the path? This is Paul's concern all the way through the letter (1:6, 19; 3:7; 4:1; 5:16; 6:10; 6:21). Though riches may indeed come to those who set their heart on them, they will often be accompanied by the person becoming lukewarm in their faith and eventually wandering completely from the path. Yet that is not all, as once again for emphasis, Paul contrasts great gain with the terrible loss of these people piercing themselves with many griefs in eternity. He pictures them in torment crying out 'if only I had not loved money so much'.

In drawing out the destination of the false teachers who had embraced a form of godliness because it had led to financial gain, Paul merely proves his earlier point. Such false teachers in reality know nothing (6:4a) and have themselves been robbed of the truth (6:5b) or surely they would not have embarked on such a terrible pathway. The ultimate answer is not to focus on the present world but on what believers will receive in the coming age, through the work of Christ who will one day return and inaugurate a new day.

Combining 1:3-7 with 6:3-10 gives us a much fuller portrayal of the false teachers at Ephesus. They managed to focus on the law and to focus on material possessions – legalism and materialism. In doing so they had neglected the doctrines of grace and glory. The grace of God frees us from legalism by reminding us that it's not all about what we do that counts; it's all about what Christ has done on the cross. The glory of God frees us from materialism by reminding us that it's not all about what we have that counts; it's all about what Christ will bring when He returns in all His glory.

From text to teaching

Get the message clear

Big idea (theme)
Turning from the words of Christ will ultimately lead to eternal disaster.

Big questions (aim)
Preaching or teaching on this passage should answer the following questions:

1. What is the likely outcome for those who turn away from the words of Christ?

2. How can Christians embrace contentment whilst living in such an acquisitive society?

3. What are the spiritual dangers both now and in eternity for those who set their heart on riches?

Engage the hearer

Point of contact
Our world is driven by money and our thinking as a society is dominated by financial concerns. We are bombarded by advertisements on television which promise us better value or which seduce us into wanting more. People are concerned

about their pay and whether it is keeping up with inflation. They are concerned about where to invest and how to get a good return on their money. They worry about interest and mortgage rates. They are anxious about how much their pension will be worth. They are alarmed about price rises and job cuts. Everything is driven by money and the security and luxuries it provides. And since this is the world we inhabit, it is very easy for us as Christians to be concerned by the same things and for us to embrace the same values.

Main illustration
Dry rot is always a serious issue. Once it is present within a structure, it tends to spread, though at the start of this process is often unseen. Eventually, though, its effects become observable and if permitted to continue, it can infect the whole building and bring it down. Given its potential for such damage, it is not surprising that the best solution is either to prevent its occurrence, or to have regular inspections in order to deal quickly with any outbreak. Similarly, with false teaching within the church, though at first it may not be detected, eventually it has the capacity to spread and do untold damage to the spiritual health of the church. This passage both highlights some of the manifestations of certain aspects of false teaching and also reveals the long-term seriousness of the situation in order for us to be forewarned.

Application
It is an amazing conceit that anyone as a professing Christian could even think of rejecting the words of our Lord Jesus Christ. It is staggering that such people are in effect saying that they know more than Him! Yet such has often been

the case through the centuries. Given that the words of Jesus are described as sound or healthy, it is no wonder that a sickly, weak church results when such decisions are taken by church leaders. Of course it will be wrapped up in careful ways, e.g. by saying that Jesus' words were true then but do not apply in our modern world, or by a twisting of language in order to make the sense of His teaching different from what has been accepted down through the centuries. The reality is that a healthy church needs healthy doctrine, which comes from a full acceptance of God's Word.

Paul includes a striking image of people being robbed of the truth. It's a picture of someone being mugged in the street and being stripped of their possessions leaving them with nothing of value. That is the effect of false teaching on the church. Again, being aware of this possibility, churches need to select their leaders with great care and hold them accountable for their teaching. In many churches and denominations there are few if any such controls, which should be a cause of great concern. No wonder Paul warned the Ephesian church leaders with tears (Acts 20:29-31); so concerned was he about the damage that could be done by false teachers.

The centre of paragraph 6:3-5 could be used as a diagnostic tool in many fellowships. Within the church family is there evidence of quarrels, malicious or constant friction? Though no fellowship is perfect and all are sinners, nevertheless it is sometimes good to assess our corporate behaviour in order to bring our beliefs and behaviour back in line with Scripture.

Genuine contentment is a beautiful fruit of the Spirit in the life of a believer and is profoundly counter-cultural. Our society is constantly offering and demanding more, as evidenced in advertising commercials. We have become ever more materialistic, acquisitive and consumerist, defining our lives by what we have or own. It all feeds into our greed and desire for more. The believer however has great riches both now and in eternity and it is only as we recognise these things that we will begin to learn true Christian contentment. Contentment in Christ has its own value for the believer, but in the rush and eagerness to get more, which characterises our society, it is also a powerful witness to the sufficiency of Christ.

Feeding the desire to get rich simply feeds other desires. This is why, strangely enough, wealth does not bring lasting happiness. Of course wealth can provide temporary benefits for our enjoyment, but these very pleasures, according to Paul, can be a trap that ensnares people. Wealth promises happiness and freedom from worry, but it cannot deliver and brings with it its own concerns and anxieties. It is desperately sad to see people completely over-stretched financially who have fallen into this trap of wanting more and more, but who have found that this appetite can never be satisfied.

Even worse is the description in 6:10 of those who have wandered from the faith through their love of money. Jesus was correct in his warning to the disciples after meeting the rich, young man that it is hard for a rich man to enter the Kingdom of God (see Mark 10:21-23). One of the dangers for believers is that their commendable work ethic as they serve Christ may lead to promotions and higher salaries. Yet, with these benefits often comes a decline in genuine Christian commitment and it is sadly no surprise when they eventually wander off from the church. Rarely is it that there is any fundamental problem in belief, though that may often be the smokescreen. Rather, it is like the situation described in Mark 4:18, 19 concerning the seed amongst thorns which was eventually choked by 'the worries of this life, the deceitfulness of wealth and the desires for other things'. As will be seen later in looking at 6:17-19 there is nothing wrong with money in itself, but the way in which it is used reveals whether Jesus is really our Lord or not.

Proclaiming the message/suggestions for preaching

A preaching outline

Title: **The danger of turning away from the word of Christ**

Text: **1 Timothy 6:3-10**

1. Rejecting the word of Christ (6:3-5)

   + The content of the false teaching (6:3, 5c)

   + The reality of the situation (6:4a, 5b)

   + The results of their teaching (6:4b, 5a)

2. Accepting the love of money (6:6-10)

   + The path of contentment (6:6-8)

   + The path of craving for more (6:9, 10)

Other preaching possibilities:
In the light of the structure of this section (6:3-21) it would be perfectly possible to preach on the whole chapter in the following way:

The danger of false teaching (6:3-10)

1. Putting our trust in what we can get now (3-5)

2. The consequences of loving money (6-10)

    a.   The antidote to false teaching (6:11-19)

         ✦   Putting our trust in what Christ will give us (11-16)

         ✦   Using money for eternal gain (17-19)

    b.   The challenge to Timothy (6:20, 21)

The advantage of handling the material in this way is that it helps to see the overview of the section and especially enables our hearers to see how the two sections on money fit together within Paul's argument. It also enables the descriptions of how Timothy is to act to be seen in the context of the threats to the church that they posed. The downside is that there is much material to cover and this may make the preacher hesitate to proceed down this route.

Another possibility is to look at the material in 1 Timothy 6 on money apart from, or at the end of, a series. The danger with such a topical sermon is that it is possible to wrench passages out of context and that is easily done here. However, once the preliminary expository preparation has been done so that the preacher is clear about the context, preaching the occasional topical sermon may be very useful. The following outline may be of assistance:

1.   The wrong attitude to money

    ✦   Desiring more and more (6:9, 10)

    ✦   Investing in oneself (6:17)

2.   The correct attitude to money

    ✦   Contentment with what you have (6:6-8)

    ✦   Investing in the future (6:18, 19)

Leading a Bible Study

Title: **The danger of turning away from the word of Christ**

Text: **1 Timothy 6:3-10**

1. Introduce the issues:

   + In what ways do we see people around us, and ourselves, ensnared by riches or the desire for wealth?

2. Study the passage

   + Why is the action of 6:3 described as being conceited or arrogant? (6:3, 4)

   + How is it possible for people to be robbed of the truth and what are the consequences? (6:4, 5)

   + What is the secret of genuine Christian contentment? (6:6-8)

   + How do verses 9 and 10 explain, in differing but similar ways, what happens when contentment is lacking? (6:9, 10)

   + What sort of things in 1 Timothy cause people to wander from the faith? (see 1:6; 4:1f; 5:15; 6:10; 6:21)

   + What is the 'great gain' of 6:6 and what is the corresponding 'great loss' described in 6:9, 10?

3. Think it through

   + How is it best to deal with friction within the church when it develops? (6:3-5)

   + What are the marks which show whether a Christian is truly content? (6:6-8)

+ Describe some of the traps which people fall into when they want to get rich. (6:9)

+ In what ways have you observed the love of money being ruinous for someone's faith in Christ? (6:10)

4. Live it out

+ How can we encourage each other to be more content and avoid a love for money?

+ What are the things which will help us not to wander from the faith?

2. Living in the light of Christ's return (6:11-21)

Introduction

Paul brings this epistle to a close and in doing so seeks to accomplish a number of things. First, he concludes the section which began at 6:3 by providing Timothy with a contrast between the false teachers and the genuine article. Not only does he compare the fruit of these respective ministries, but he also highlights the difference that a true perspective on issues of wealth and handling money will lead to. At each point, in contrast to the immediacy of the false teachers' concerns, Paul encourages Timothy to live in the light of the return of Christ and the coming age. By this means, Timothy and the church will receive encouragement and a sense of direction even amidst the pressures and challenges that they face.

In the last two verses of the epistle (already briefly considered alongside 1:1-7 in the opening exposition), the apostle gives his final appeal to Timothy. In doing so, he sums up many of the main themes of the whole book whilst also mirroring the challenge that came at the end of the first section (1:18-20).

Listening to the text

Context, structure and observations

Context

The phrase 'but you' at 6:11 shows that there is a clear connection and contrast with the preceding material in this section. It reveals that 6:11-19 cannot be understood properly without being rooted in the context of 6:3-10, whilst it also helps us to see Paul's particular concerns in relation to how Timothy is to face this threat. This personal element in charging Timothy with certain tasks is developed at the end of the section (see 6:20, 21) which, like the end of the first section (see 1:18-20), sees Paul bring a personal and direct challenge to his protégé.

Structure

The structure of the whole section 6:3-21 has already been referred to in the previous exposition. Looking simply at the passage 6:11-21 there are three obvious sections:

1. Instructions to Timothy 6:11-16

2. Handling wealth 6:17-19

3. Instructions to Timothy 6:20, 21

The portion concerning handling wealth may at first glance look out of place but in fact it is carefully linked to the preceding verses by means of a common theme and some significant shared vocabulary. Further, it mirrors the position of 6:6-10 in revealing how the handling of money reflects the teaching that has been received.

Observations

It is helpful to look at the internal links within this passage. First, within 6:17-19 there is a fourfold repetition of the word for wealth or riches which clearly identifies the theme of the verses. Second, these verses are linked to the previous passage by the phrase 'take hold of life' which appears at 6:12 and 6:19. In context this is eternal life and points to the future experience of life in the coming age, indicating a coming together of the focus in 6:11-16 and 6:17-19. This is further underlined by the fact that life comes through putting one's hope in God or Christ (1:1; 4:10; 6:15, 17) and from this we see the whole future orientation of the section. Whereas in combating the legalism of the false teachers Paul appealed to the finished work of Christ on the cross, here in combating the materialism of the false teachers Paul appeals to the future work of Christ in returning and ushering in the coming age.

It is also of great importance to notice the many links between this section 6:3-21 and the first section 1:1-20. In the last exposition we noted that the apostle makes specific reference to those teaching false doctrines (1:3; 6:3) which led to controversies and arguments (1:4; 6:4), but now we see many other verbal links which serve to tie the whole letter together. In both sections Timothy receives a solemn charge which is repeated (1:3, 18; 6:13, 20). This charge is to 'fight the good fight' (1:18; 6:12), indicating the reality of the spiritual battle. In both sections, Paul gets carried along in his argument and ends up in doxologies (1:17; 6:15, 16) which share many common features. There is also the concern expressed that, due to the false teaching, people are wandering from the faith (1:6; 6:21). In all these ways we can see that Paul is returning to his opening theme, though developing it further.

Finally, it is also worth identifying the theme of godly living leading to a life of love and good works, which has been a dominant characteristic of the whole letter. The importance of love is mentioned at the beginning, middle and end (1:5; 4:12; 6:11), whilst in the second and fourth sections of the letter it is either specifically mentioned (2:15) or implied in the qualities expected within the church family and its leaders. The theme of good works, which will also serve to enhance the reputation of the church and the gospel, also recurs regularly as well as at the end of the letter (2:10; 5:10; 5:25 and 6:18). If the negative challenge is for Timothy to deal with the false teachers, the positive encouragement is for him and the whole church family to embrace a life of love towards others and to be rich in good deeds which will serve to put the gospel on display within the world.

Exposition
Using the structure of the passage already identified there are three main parts which need to be developed:

Living in the light of Christ's return (6:11-16)
Paul starts with the strong 'but you', which shows that this is a personal address to Timothy by way of contrast with the false teachers already identified earlier at 6:3. Timothy is further identified as 'man of God'. This could be a general reference which might equally apply to all Christians, but, particularly within this context, it is linked with its Old Testament usage where it specifically refers to the leader of God's people by identifying God's servant (e.g. see the superscription to Psalm 90 or the many references to Elijah and Elisha in 2 Kings). This is likely to be the case because Paul is drawing a contrast between the false teachers of 6:3 and the true servant of the Lord. In order to do this, Paul strengthens Timothy by this reminder that he is the 'man of

God' charged with the role, like Elijah and Elisha in their day, of confronting those who would seek to lead God's people astray. So, what is Paul expecting Timothy to do?

Understand your present position (6:11, 12a)
First, Timothy must understand the particular pressures that have arisen due to the false teachers and these should help to focus his mind on how to respond. As the leader of God's people, he must flee, follow and fight.

1. Flee (6:11a)
'Flee from all this' refers to the teaching and behaviour of the false teachers (6:3-5) and particularly the way their views had shaped their handling of money, giving rein to greater desires for wealth at the cost of their faith (6:6-10). Pride, in the form of conceit (6:4), and greed, in the form of their love of money (6:10), are to be avoided above all by Timothy.

2. Follow (6:11b)
Instead of this, Timothy, as leader of God's people, is to follow or pursue a very different route. It is the way of love highlighted at the beginning as the aim of God's work (1:5) and referred to in a similar list applicable to Timothy at 4:12. It is the way of godliness which has been one of the central themes of the letter (see 2:2, 15 ;3:16; 4:8). It is interesting to note that, though Paul's specific issue concerns the need to resist the false teachers, this is prefaced by the need for Timothy to demonstrate appropriate Christian conduct as one who leads within God's household. It is going to be as much the manner in which Timothy operates as what he does which will be of critical importance. Hence there is the need for gentleness alongside qualities such as endurance in the struggle for the leadership of the church.

It will not be an easy, quick battle, which is why Timothy will need endurance; but, in entering the fray, Timothy must remain an example of godliness and so it will be particularly important to demonstrate gentleness. These things Timothy is to follow or pursue, putting all his energy into the pursuit.

3. Fight (6:12)

These instructions come to a climax with the command for Timothy to fight the good fight of the faith. As at 1:18 there will be a battle for the church over what is correct doctrine as opposed to what is false (6:3). Satan has been mentioned at various points within the letter directly or indirectly (e.g. 1:20; 2:14; 3:6, 7; 4:1; 5:15) and he is determined to cause people, especially church leaders, to abandon or make shipwreck of their faith. Timothy cannot excuse himself from this spiritual battle but must, for the sake of the gospel, be fully engaged in it, so that the church continues to be a pillar of the truth (3:15).

Remember your future situation (6:12b-15a)
Moving now from the present, Paul reminds Timothy of the eternal perspective. This should powerfully encourage him in the struggle (6:12b).

1. Take hold (6:12b)

All this is to be done with a clear eye on the future held out for Timothy and indeed for every believer. At Timothy's conversion, when he committed to following Christ, which may have been publicly witnessed when he was baptised shortly afterwards, he took hold of the prospect of eternal life. That life is a reality in this age but it is to be fully experienced in the coming age. Having set his course, Timothy is now to hold on and not permit himself to be distracted, even though the struggle for the church might involve great difficulty and even suffering. He is to hold on to this future reality, which is equivalent to salvation itself (see 4:16).

2.   Take heart (6:13)

Having mentioned the witnesses present around the time of Timothy's conversion or baptism, Paul reminds Timothy of other witnesses around to encourage him to take heart and to hold on in this journey (6:13). He is to remember that he stands in the presence of the God who gives life and who will sustain him all the way. He is also to remember that he stands in the presence of the Lord Jesus Christ, who has walked the same road before him, enduring suffering before Pontius Pilate when He testified to the truth, knowing by faith that His suffering would be followed by resurrection life. As at Hebrews 12:1, Jesus endured the cross, scorning its shame because of the joy set before Him. At the point of suffering and death Jesus had complete confidence in God and it is this same Jesus now at the right hand of the Father who should be an encouragement when Timothy is called to walk in the same path. These divine witnesses should be an enormous encouragement to Timothy in the battle, reminding him that he will indeed get to the finishing line whatever the obstacles.

3.   Take comfort (6:14, 15a)

But how long must Timothy hold on for amidst all these pressures? He is to do so until the appearing of our Lord Jesus Christ which will be brought about by God in His own time (6:14, 15a). This will be the great day that ushers in the life that is truly life (see 6:19) and which will bring an end to all suffering and struggles. No wonder Paul started the whole letter by referring to God our Saviour and Christ our hope, since the work of Christ on the cross and His final appearing mark and define the span of our labours in this age as Christians. We live as those saved by grace through the cross of Christ and we work until He returns and ushers in the new heavens and the new earth.

This return is not an uncertain event but one that can be guaranteed (though on God's timetable, not ours) which should provide encouragement, confidence and enormous comfort in the present. Everything Timothy does therefore is to be done in the light of the return of Christ. The reference to the return of Christ is not just a mark that the finishing line has come; instead it is referred to as the appearing of our Lord Jesus Christ. It is this that Timothy is to look forward to, as it will be the day when he will see the one who died for him. In contrast to those at 6:3 who are rejecting the words of Jesus, Timothy will hear words from the Lord Himself, directly from His mouth. Then he will finally have experienced salvation, along with God's people, in its very richest sense as he is welcomed into glory.

In other words, whereas the false teachers have lost sight of the future and therefore live only for this world and for the satisfaction of their immediate desires, Timothy is to keep his eyes firmly on the future reality of the appearing of Christ such that this should encourage him and shape the way he lives in the present.

Give glory to God (6:15b, 16)

As at 1:17, Paul cannot help but turn to praise God. In the opening section it was thinking of the cross of Christ and the overflowing grace of God that led to his overflow of praise. Here, with very similar terminology, it is reference to the final appearing of Christ, which God will bring about, which causes Paul to arrive at this pinnacle of praise and adoration. Again, the contrast with the false teachers is unmistakable. The fruit of their ministry is angry words amongst each other (6:4, 5a), whereas the fruit of Paul's ministry is words of adoration spoken directly to God.

With regard to the descriptions of God that are used, Paul focuses on the fact that God is both the only Ruler and that He is unseen, living in unapproachable light. As the only Sovereign, He is 'King of kings' and 'Lord of lords' who will therefore achieve all His purposes. As a result, the Christian can live in contentment (see 6:6-8) knowing that everything is in good hands. In contrast to the false teachers fixing their eyes on what is seen – money and wealth (6:5, 9, 10) – believers are to fix their eyes on the unseen God whom they know by faith (see 1:4) and who will one day be revealed in splendour, when Christ appears in all His glory.

This important passage is centred on the appearing of the Lord Jesus Christ and Timothy is to live in the light of this return. This should strengthen, encourage and comfort him as he struggles against the false teachers.

How the future should shape the present (6:17-19)
As in the previous passage (6:3-10), Paul demonstrates the outworking of a theological position by reference to how it affects one's attitude to money. It is a litmus test which exposes the degree to which the gospel message has really taken root in our lives. The fact that the false teachers and those who imbibed their teaching were so eager for financial gain betrayed the fact that these people were only focusing on the present. In contrast, Paul wants to see money and wealth being used productively now in the light of eternity. In these verses he outlines one of the ways in which Timothy can take hold of eternal life (6:12), which is through using wealth with an eye to the future (6:19).

Something to avoid in this present age (6:17a)

Paul started his warning to the false teachers about their attitudes to money by giving a contrasting picture of Christian contentment (6:6-10). Here he reverses the procedure and before outlining the right attitude to the use of wealth, he highlights the pitfalls to be avoided which perhaps some of the congregation had already fallen into. So those who have financial riches in this present age are not to be arrogant, thinking that their wealth might necessarily be a sign of their abilities or even of God's blessing on them. Their arrogance will soon be exposed as they continue on the slippery slope described earlier at 6:9, 10. Neither are they to set their hope on riches, precisely because though it looks so important, it is uncertain. Jesus highlights this in his parable of the Rich Fool who plans to build bigger barns to store his crops. 'But God said to him "You fool! This very night your life will be demanded from you. Then who will get what you have prepared for yourself?"'(Luke 12:20) We have also seen this powerfully demonstrated in various stock market crashes over the years, where the stability apparently provided by wealth has suddenly been discovered to be illusory, so that trusting in certain investments has actually been more akin to building on sinking sand. Though wealth promises so much, ultimately it provides no security – sometimes in this life, certainly in the next.

Something to aim for in the light of the coming age (6:17b-19)

In contrast to the warnings in the first part of the verse, believers are to put their hope or confidence in God. There need be no uncertainty about this because of who He is, described so vividly in the previous verses (6:15, 16). Given that He is the Sovereign One, Creator and Redeemer, He has given us all things richly to enjoy. Perhaps there is a glancing blow to some of the ascetics within the church leadership who had forbidden people to marry and to eat certain foods (4:3). Rather than being a killjoy, developing restrictions and rules, God has lavishly provided a wonderful creation and glorious redemption. Here are great riches. Paul starts then with a recognition of the sheer generosity of God to help us in thinking through our attitude to wealth.

Yet this wealth, though coming from God's hand, is to be used in accordance with the principles already set out within 1 Timothy. Rich people, like all believers within Ephesus, are to do good and they are to strive to be rich in good works. This is the sign that the gospel of Christ has taken hold in someone's life, when they become known within the church and the wider community for their good works (e.g. 2:2, 10; 5:10, 25). And within the context of Paul's current concern with the issue of handling wealth, these good works will certainly include financial generosity and a willingness to share (6:18). Again, within the wider context of the letter, Paul is envisaging rich Christians providing practical support for the widows in their own family (5:7, 8) and for those on the church list (5:9) as well as supporting the church leadership appropriately (5:17, 18). The generosity of God should lead inevitably to the generosity of believers as we are shaped more and more into His image.

In contrast to the flimsy, uncertain foundations that others may build on in this present age as they hold on to their wealth, the believers who are generous with what God has generously given to them will discover that they are constructing a firm foundation for the coming age. In giving away riches in this world they will be storing up treasure in the next. The good works of the believer are of enormous value now, both for the church and for the reputation of the church in the world, but they also yield a wonderful dividend in the future, at the appearing of our Lord Jesus Christ. This is the way, says Paul, by which rich people can take hold of life which is truly life; life which in context is the life of the coming age (6:19).

Once again, Paul has given a worked example of how the handling of money reveals the core of our faith. Within these three verses, riches and their use reveal Paul's emphasis on God as Creator and Redeemer and on Christians as those who should seek to use what they have for the benefit of others through good works. Whereas the legalism and materialism of the false teachers had focussed on rules, self-denial and the selfish use of riches which issued in controversies and friction, Paul's vision for Timothy and the church at Ephesus is for believers to delight in God's riches in creation and redemption. This should issue in generosity and good works flooding out from God's household, thus displaying the truth even more clearly to the world (3:15). All this is crystallised by the coming appearance of our Lord Jesus Christ, who will expose what we have been building our life upon and who will grant to those who have put their faith in God as Saviour, and their hope in Christ as Lord (see 1:1), the life that is truly life.

Living in the light of current danger (6:20, 21)
Although these two verses have already been briefly considered alongside the opening exposition (1:1-7) it is appropriate to look at them also within the context of the final section of the letter (6:3-21). This section begins and ends with reference to the false teachers (6:3, 21) and is to be seen in the light of the current struggle going on within

the church. Paul launches his final appeal to Timothy by reminding him of two things:

Guard the gospel (6:20a)
What has been entrusted to Paul (1:11ff) and has been entrusted to Timothy is the gospel message, which in the context of 1 Timothy, includes both the message itself and its outworking in the lives of believers in godliness. This is a great treasure in its own right and leads to further treasures (see 6:19) as people hear this message and embrace it and are transformed. Given how valuable all this is, it is no wonder that Paul calls for Timothy to guard this deposit. In the same way that, if you are entrusted with the care of a neighbour's property whilst they are away on holiday, you would do all you could to prevent a burglar from seizing any valuable possessions, so Timothy is to guard the gospel from those who would seek to take away its treasures. Through the actions of the false teachers, the congregation has been robbed of the truth (6:5) but Timothy must do everything he can to stop it happening whilst he is in charge. Though Paul has already warned the church leaders at Ephesus to be on their guard against wolves coming to savage the flock (Acts 20:29-31), the command had not been heeded sufficiently and as a result it falls to Timothy to do this job of preserving the gospel treasure against further attacks.

Avoid error (6:20b, 21)
The other side of the coin is that guarding the gospel will involve avoiding the path of the false teachers. They had turned away from the words of Christ (6:3) and embraced godless chatter and so-called 'knowledge', but these were the very means of leading people to wander from the faith. As opposed to the clarity of holding on to life (6:12, 19) we

have the image of letting go and wandering off the path. Given this context, Timothy must see how important it is that he commits himself to guarding the faith.

So, right at the end of the epistle is the summary of the main themes which add clarity and urgency to the role mapped out for Timothy.

The final task for Paul is to commit the whole church family, including Timothy, to God's grace. As at Miletus, speaking to the church leaders, Paul commits them to the word of his grace, knowing that this is able to build them up and give them an inheritance (Acts 20:32). By grace an inheritance is available to the church through the work of the crucified yet returning Saviour, our Lord Jesus Christ, whose grace continues to overflow abundantly.

From text to teaching

Get the message clear

Big idea (theme)
We are to live in the light of the appearing of our Lord Jesus Christ.

Big questions (aim)
Preaching or teaching on this passage should answer the following questions:

1. In what ways should the doctrine of the return of Christ shape and inspire Christian ministry?

2. How should Christians be using their money and wealth?

3. What is involved in guarding the gospel and why is it so important?

Engage the hearer

Point of contact

Our thinking has often been that the future is uncertain and therefore the most prudent thing to do is to build up savings and investment. These will provide the security that is required. Clearly stock market crashes and other financial difficulties have punctured this view to a certain extent, but it is still our natural fallback position. The teaching here completely reverses that position so that genuine certainty is found in the future in the coming age with God.

Main illustration

When moving house to a different location, perhaps with a different climate, you will often find that the future has a real impact on the present. If the furniture in the first house is simply far too large for the next one then there is no point transferring it. Equally, if there are particular items that seem essential for the new house, then the cost may be paid in the present, even though there is no instant benefit. A similar analogy could be used in terms of going on holiday. Different clothes and appropriate currency are purchased, ready for use in the future. These are simply illustrations concerning the way that living in the light of return of Christ should affect the present for the believer.

Application

Christian leaders need to have a clear focus in their ministry and cannot afford to drift. The commands to flee, follow and fight should inject in all leaders a note of urgency and determination in the way in which they live and conduct their ministry. As many ministers work alone and have considerable practical responsibilities and perhaps a lower than average salary, temptations relating to money can easily arise. They are to flee from such temptations and the church should assist in this task by paying them appropriately (5:17, 18). Preachers who have been believers for many years can also reach a plateau in their discipleship, settling into their usual habits and responses. Instead they are to follow and pursue the qualities referred to at 6:11 until they are attained and the church family can help by praying regularly for them. Pastors can easily get worn down by the battles within the church for orthodoxy, because of their time-consuming nature and the unpleasantness of having to confront unorthodox views. However, each one is called to play their part in the spiritual battle and again the fellowship can help by standing firmly alongside their minister in such circumstances.

As believers we need to find ways of strengthening our grip on the future in order to sustain us in the present. We need to spend much time in the Scriptures gaining comfort from the fact that we serve the living God, who will be faithful to all His promises and all His people. We are to meditate on the way Jesus faced suffering and the cross as an example to us, so that we also might emerge to resurrection life. We are, above all, to look forward to the day when the Lord Jesus Christ will appear. Such hope and confidence should give us renewed strength now.

Our knowledge of God should also provide us with enormous encouragement. As we contemplate the fact that God is the Sovereign ruler over all, we should be able to learn greater trust and contentment even amidst the struggles of life. True worship will be expressed in delighting in all the different attributes of the Lord and letting those truths shape and direct us in ways that please Him. Perhaps we need to ask ourselves the question whether, like Paul in this passage, we have been so captivated by thoughts of God that our hearts have overflowed in praise?

Putting our trust in riches is indeed an uncertain business and yet that is the way our society works. We need to expose the folly of this sort of thinking and remind people of the fragility of the foundation that so many are building on. By way of contrast, as Christians we should be able, through the way we live our lives and handle our money, to show where we think our true treasure is. How tragic it is when our non-Christian friends can see no difference at all in this area and where our Christianity has made no impact on our materialistic and consumerist mindset. Are we known for our generosity and willingness to share?

Christian leaders are called to guard the faith. Within the Church of England there are clear and strong words promised by those ordained to guard the truth and defend the flock and yet so often it means very little indeed. Guards outside royal palaces often perform a purely ceremonial role, but that is not to be the case for those standing guard over the flock of Christ. Ministers have been entrusted with something of tremendous value and must therefore endeavour to protect it.

Proclaiming the message/suggestions for preaching

A preaching outline

Title: **Living in the light of Christ's return**

Text: **1 Timothy 6:11-21**

1. Living in the light of Christ's return (6:11-16)

    a. Understand your present position (6:11,12a)

    ✦ flee (6:11a)

    ✦ follow (6:11b)

    ✦ fight (6:12a)

   b.   Remember your future destination (6:12b-15a)

- take hold (6:12b)

- take heart (6:13)

- take comfort (6:14,15a)

   c.   Give glory to God (6:15b, 16)

2. How the future should shape the present (6:17-19)

- Something to avoid in this present age (6:17a)

- Something to aim for in the light of the coming age (6:17b-19)

3. Living in the light of the current danger (6:20, 21)

- Guard the gospel (6:20a)

- Avoid error (6:20b, 21)

Other preaching possibilities:
Some of the other preaching possibilities have already been considered. In covering 1 Timothy 6:3-10 it was suggested that it would be possible to consider the whole section (6:3-21) because of its common theme and clear structure. Further, a topical sermon on the subject of money based on 6:6-10 and 6:17-19 would be possible, though attention would need to be given to the context.

Another possibility in speaking to those in church leadership would be to consider 6:11-16 and the call to flee, follow, fight and hold on to the future hope.

One final suggestion would be to finish off a preaching series by considering 6:20, 21 its own. The advantage is that it would be possible to draw in several of the key issues within the letter, in order to provide both an overview and a summary of the whole.

Leading a Bible Study
Title: **Living in the light of Christ's return**
Text: **1 Timothy 6:11-21**

1. Introduce the issues

    +   In what different ways is our society dominated by a concern for the immediate as opposed to being concerned for the future?

2. Study the passage

    +   What should Timothy flee from and what should he be pursuing and why? (6:11)

    +   What is involved in fighting the good fight of the faith and how should it be done? (6:11, 12)

    +   What encouragements does Paul give to Timothy in this struggle? (6:12-16)

    +   What are the dangers for those who are rich? (6:17)

    +   How are we to store up genuine riches? (6:18, 19)

    +   What will guarding what was entrusted to Timothy mean in practice and why is it so important? (6:20, 21)

3. Think it through

    +   What are the warning signs that a minister is not fulfilling Paul's call in 6:11, 12?

    +   To what extent should the future appearing of Christ shape the way that you live? (6:13-16)

    +   What do you think might be involved for you in storing up treasures for the coming age? (6:12-19)

+ In your experience, what are the reasons why some people do wander from the faith? (6:20, 21)

4. Live it out

+ How could the certainty of the future appearing of Christ shape my behaviour and decisions this week?

+ How can we encourage each other to be the sort of people described in 6:18?

FURTHER READING

Introduction

This book is not a commentary in the sense of fully expounding the text of 1 Timothy and giving detailed justification for all the interpretations suggested. Nor is it a series of sermons on 1 Timothy. Rather, it gives guidance and encouragement to those who want to preach the message of 1 Timothy, but are uncertain how to go about it. There are many commentaries on 1 Timothy, often alongside 2 Timothy and Titus in the Pastoral Epistles, and the purpose of this brief chapter is to give guidance on some which I have found useful and stimulating, both in preaching through 1 Timothy myself as well as in researching this book. It should be remembered that no single commentary will be helpful on every passage. However, commentaries can provide enormous assistance in helping us to understand the text accurately so that we can expound it effectively. Below are some suggestions with brief comments which may help in assessing whether or not a particular resource would be useful to you.

Commentaries on 1 Timothy

It is worth considering having one larger commentary which can assist with most of the finer details. I have benefited considerably both from the Word Commentary on the Pastoral Epistles by William D. Mounce (Nashville, Nelson, 2000) and the New International Greek Testament Commentary on the Pastoral Epistles by George W. Knight III (Carlisle, Paternoster, 1992). Both hold to Paul's authorship of these letters and follow a conservative traditional interpretation on passages such as 1 Timothy 2:11-15. Both can be used without knowledge of Greek, though clearly even a cursory knowledge of the original language is extremely helpful when using these commentaries. My slight preference would be to use Mounce because his commentary is fuller, more detailed and he engages more thoroughly with other interpretations. However, either would be extremely useful for the preacher who wishes to spend time digging through the text as thoroughly as possible.

Two other larger commentaries which are worth considering are not as conservative, but nevertheless are full of helpful details and insights. They are the International Critical Commentary on the Pastoral Epistles by I. Howard Marshall (Edinburgh, T & T Clark, 1999) and the Critical Eerdmans Commentary on 1 and 2 Timothy by Jerome D. Quinn and William C. Wacker (Grand Rapids, Eerdmans, 2000). Though I found myself disagreeing with a number of interpretations, both commentaries are meticulous in handling a range of issues and are enormously stimulating.

It is also well worth getting hold of a shorter commentary and the one I found really helpful was the New International Biblical Commentary on the Pastoral Epistles by Gordon D. Fee (Peabody, Henrickson, 1984). Fee consistently seeks to set the letter in its historical context and enables the preacher to get a really good understanding of the flow of the epistle. The Tyndale Commentary by Donald Guthrie (Leicester, IVP, 1957) is very helpful on the issue of Pauline authorship though perhaps less helpful in his exegesis in comparison to Fee or the larger commentaries. As usual, the contribution to the Bible Speaks Today series by John R.W. Stott on 1 Timothy and Titus (Leicester, IVP, 1996) is enormously helpful in providing clear and lucid insights which are of particular benefit to the preacher.

Clearly, it is not possible to read everything and decisions need to be made concerning how much time you have or can make available. The preacher will want to remember that, though understanding the text is absolutely vital, yet it is only one stage in the journey to preaching a message to God's people which will encourage, strengthen, teach, train, correct and rebuke. Sometimes one commentary will help to unlock the meaning whilst another will help you to think through issues of application.

If you have decided to embark on an expository series on 1 Timothy my own suggestion would be to obtain either Mounce or Knight together with Fee or Stott.

1 Timothy 2:9-15

Obviously there is considerable controversy on this passage and a range of interpretations. For further assistance, the preacher may find help from two particularly useful resources. *Women in the Church – a fresh analysis of 1 Timothy 2:9-15* edited by Andreas J. Köstenberger, Thomas R. Schreiner and H. Scott Baldwin (Grand Rapids, Baker Book House, 1995) is extremely meticulous and thorough in considering the text from a number of different angles. There is also a helpful essay by Douglas J. Moo in *Recovering Biblical*

Manhood and Womanhood edited by John Piper and Wayne Grudem (Wheaton, Crossway, 1991) which looks in detail at this passage. Further assistance from this conservative viewpoint is provided by Wayne Grudem in *Evangelical Feminism and Biblical Truth* (Leicester, Apollos, 2004), where he interacts with a whole range of questions, some of which relate specifically to 1 Timothy 2:9-15. To see how those not convinced by this complementarian position handle the passage you could consult *Discovering Biblical Equality* edited by Ronald W. Pierce, Rebecca Merrill Groothuis and Gordon D. Fee (Leicester, Apollos, 2004).

Audio Resources

Nowadays there are many opportunities to hear how others have preached 1 Timothy through CD, MP3 or the worldwide web. Dick Lucas preached a particularly helpful series under the auspices of the Proclamation Trust on 1 Timothy which can be located on the Proclamation Trust website 'Instructions on 1 Timothy'. The Gospel Coalition website also carries a large number of sermons on passages in 1 Timothy. Such sermons can be educative and provide good insights on applying the text. However, there is the danger that preachers will simply repeat what they have heard without wrestling with the Biblical texts themselves. Only as the Word of God dwells richly within the preacher will it start to make an impact on the life of the preacher and in turn on these who hear. As Paul states at 1 Timothy 5:17, 18, hard labour is involved in the work of preaching and teaching and there are no shortcuts, though the fact that such work done well deserves 'double honour' (5:17) reminds us of the wonderful privilege of being called to this ministry.

PT RESOURCES

RESOURCES FOR PREACHERS AND BIBLE TEACHERS

PT Resources, a ministry of The Proclamation Trust, provides a range of multimedia resources for preachers and Bible teachers.

Teach the Bible Series (Christian Focus & PT Resources)
The Teaching the Bible Series, published jointly with *Christian Focus Publications*, is written by preachers, for preachers, and is specifically geared to the purpose of God's Word – its proclamation as living truth. Books in the series aim to help the reader move beyond simply understanding a text to communicating and applying it.

Current titles include: *Teaching 1 Peter, Teaching 1 Timothy, Teaching Acts, Teaching Amos, Teaching Ephesians, Teaching Isaiah, Teaching Matthew, Teaching Romans, and Teaching the Christian Hope.*

Forthcoming titles include: *Teaching Daniel, Teaching Mark, Teaching Numbers, Teaching Nehemiah and Teaching 1&2 Samuel.*

DVD Training

Preaching & Teaching the Old Testament:
   4 DVDs – Narrative, Prophecy, Poetry, Wisdom

Preaching & Teaching the New Testament
   3 DVDs – Gospels, Letters, Acts & Revelation

These training DVDs aim to give preachers and teachers confidence in handling the rich variety of God's Word. David Jackman has taught this material to generations of Cornhill students, and gives us step-by-step instructions on handling each genre of biblical literature.

He demonstrates principles that will guide us through the challenges of teaching and applying different parts of the Bible, for example:

- How does prophecy relate to the lives of its hearers – ancient and modern?
- How can you preach in a way that reflects the deep emotion of the psalms?

Both sets are suitable for preachers and for those teaching the Bible in a wide variety of contexts.

- Designed for **individual** and **group** study
- Interactive learning through many **worked examples** and **exercises**
- Flexible format ideal for **training courses**
- Optional **English subtitles** for second-language users
- Print as many **workbooks** as you need (PDF)

Audio
PT Resources has a large range of Mp3 downloads, nearly all of which are entirely free to download and use.

Preaching Instruction
This series aims to help the preacher or teacher understand, open up and teach individual books of the Bible by getting to grips with their central message and purpose.

Sermon Series
These sermons, examples of great preaching, not only demonstrate faithful biblical preaching but will also refresh and instruct the hearer.

Conferences
Recordings of our conferences include challenging topical addresses, discussion of preaching and ministry issues, and warm-hearted exposition that will challenge and inspire all those in ministry.

ABOUT THE PROCLAMATION TRUST

We exist to promote church-based expository Bible ministry and especially to equip and encourage Biblical expository preachers because we recognise the primary role of preaching in God's sovereign purposes in the world through the local church.

Biblical (the message)
We believe the Bible is God's written Word and that, by the work of the Holy Spirit, as it is faithfully preached God's voice is truly heard.

Expository (the method)
Central to the preacher's task is correctly handling the Bible, seeking to discern the mind of the Spirit in the passage being expounded through prayerful study of the text in the light of its context in the biblical book and the Bible as a whole. This divine message must then be preached in dependence on the Holy Spirit to the minds, hearts and wills of the contemporary hearers.

Preachers (the messengers)
The public proclamation of God's Word by suitably gifted leaders is fundamental to a ministry that honours God, builds the church and reaches the world. God uses weak jars of clay in this task who need encouragement to persevere in their biblical convictions, ministry of God's Word and godly walk with Christ.
  We achieve this through:

+ PT Cornhill: a one year full-time or two-year part-time church based training course

+ PT Conferences: offering practical encouragement for Bible preachers, teachers and ministers' wives

+ PT Resources: including books, online resources, the PT blog (www.theproclaimer.org.uk) and podcasts

Other titles from
Christian Focus and PT Resources

Teaching 1 Peter
ISBN 978-1-84550-347-5

Teaching 1 Timothy
ISBN 978-1-84550-808-1

Teaching Acts
ISBN 978-1-84550-255-3

Teaching Amos
ISBN 978-1-84550-142-6

Teaching Ephesians
ISBN 978-1-84550-684-1

Teaching Isaiah
ISBN 978-1-84550-565-3

Teaching John
ISBN 978-1-85792-790-0

Teaching Matthew
ISBN 978-1-84550-480-9

Teaching Romans (volume 1)
ISBN 978-1-84550-455-7

Teaching Romans (volume 2)
ISBN 978-1-84550-456-4

Teaching the Christian Hope
ISBN 978-1-85792-518-0

Christian Focus Publications
publishes books for all ages

Our mission statement –

STAYING FAITHFUL

In dependence upon God we seek to impact the world through literature faithful to His infallible Word, the Bible. Our aim is to ensure that the LORD Jesus Christ is presented as the only hope to obtain forgiveness of sin, live a useful life and look forward to heaven with Him.

REACHING OUT

Christ's last command requires us to reach out to our world with His gospel. We seek to help fulfil that by publishing books that point people towards Jesus and help them develop a Christ-like maturity. We aim to equip all levels of readers for life, work, ministry and mission.

Books in our adult range are published in three imprints.

Christian Focus contains popular works including biographies, commentaries, basic doctrine and Christian living. Our children's books are also published in this imprint.

Mentor focuses on books written at a level suitable for Bible College and seminary students, pastors and other serious readers. The imprint includes commentaries, doctrinal studies, examination of current issues and church history.

Christian Heritage contains classic writings from the past.

Christian Focus Publications Ltd,
Geanies House, Fearn, Ross-shire,
IV20 1TW, Scotland, United Kingdom
info@christianfocus.com
www.christianfocus.com